Present	Past	Past Participle
31	fall	fell	fallen
	feed	fed	fed
	feel	felt	felt
	fight	fought	fought
	find	found	found
	flee	fled	fled
	fling	flung	flung
	fly	flew	flown
	forget	forgot	forgotten
40	freeze	froze	frozen
	get	got	got
	give	gave	given
	go	went	gone
	grind	ground	ground
	grow	grew	grown
	hang	hung	hung
	hear	heard	heard
	hide	hid	hidden
	hit	hit	hit
50	hold	held	held
	hurt	hurt	hurt
	keep	kept	kept
	kneel	knelt	knelt
	know	knew	known
	lay	laid	laid
	lead	led	led
	leave	left	left
	lend	lent	lent
	let	let	let
60	lie	lay	lain

COMMON MISTAKES IN ENGLISH
with exercises

by

T. J. FITIKIDES, B.A., F.I.L.

SENIOR ENGLISH MASTER
THE PANCYPRIAN GYMNASIUM, NICOSIA
Author of *Key Words for Easy Spelling*
Lessons in Greek-English Translation

Errors, like straws, upon the surface flow;
He who would search for pearls must dive below.
JOHN DRYDEN

LONGMAN

LONGMAN GROUP LIMITED
London

*Associated companies, branches and representatives
throughout the world*

First published 1936
Second edition 1937
Third edition 1939
Fourth edition 1947
Fifth edition 1963
*Second impression (with corrections) *1965*
*New impressions *1966; *1967; *1968; *1969;*
**1970 (twice); *1971 (thrice);*
**1972; *1973; *1974; *1975; †1976; †1977 (twice)*

ISBN 0 582 52043 6

Printed in Singapore
by Chong Moh Offset Printing Pte. Ltd.

PREFACE TO THE FIFTH EDITION

Nearly a quarter of a century has elapsed since *Common Mistakes in English* was first published. During this period several hundred thousand copies of the book have been disposed of, and, to quote the publishers, "it has sold practically in every country in the world, in fact everywhere English is taught as a second language." Nevertheless, the twenty-fifth anniversary is so important an occasion that it is being commemorated with the publication of this new edition, which has been thoroughly revised and considerably enlarged.

One hundred additional sections have been included, thus raising their number to six hundred, four times as many as were incorporated in the original edition. An important innovation is the inclusion of supplementary matter covering twelve self-contained pages, each one dealing concisely with some fundamental aspect of the language, such as the correct order of words, the use of the articles, words followed by prepositions, questions and negations. Another innovation is the introduction of a list of irregular verbs in everyday use. These verbs are intentionally placed as endpapers for easy reference.

Besides the main additions and innovations mentioned above, the opportunity has been taken of revising the book from cover to cover, bringing it up to date, and introducing many little improvements here and there.

The short paragraph in the preface to the first edition, suggesting a method of using this book, has been expanded into a fuller explanation under the heading "How the Book Should be Used", presented in the following pages. This, it is felt, should increase the usefulness of the book and, at the same time, remove any fallacious conceptions concerning the way it should be used.

T. J. F.

January 1961

PREFACE TO THE FIRST EDITION

This book has been designed to meet the requirements of students whose mother tongue is not English. Its main purpose is to help to correct the common mistakes to which foreign learners of English are liable.

The method adopted throughout this work is uniform. All the errors dealt with are singled out, for they have to be recognized before they can be corrected; then correct forms are substituted for incorrect ones; finally, simple explanations are given wherever necessary to justify particular usages. Exercises are set at the end to ensure that the principles may become firmly fixed in the students' minds.

It is not claimed that this manual is exhaustive. Nevertheless, the difficulties tackled are real, and the examples are representative of the mistakes commonly made by foreign students of English, being the result of observations made over a long period of time.

Much care has been given to the preparation of the Index, which it is hoped will make the book a useful work of reference.

My acknowledgments are due to Mr. W. H. G. Popplestone, who has read my manuscript and made many valuable suggestions.

T. J. F.

August 1936

CONTENTS

USEFUL LISTS AND SUMMARIES

HOW THE BOOK SHOULD BE USED

This book is intended for two uses. It may be used as a reference book and as an ordinary text-book.

As a book of reference it should be consulted with every composition. The teacher may refer the student to the appropriate Section dealing with his mistake by a number in the margin of his exercise book. For example, a misuse of a preposition of time (*at*, *on*, or *in*) is indicated by "393" in the margin to enable the student to look up his mistake and correct it. This method has been tested and found more effective than the common practice of writing the correct form for the student. It is axiomatic that the greater the student's individual effort, the more thorough will be his learning.

With regard to its second use, as an actual text-book, we strongly recommend that the teacher should start off with the Exercises on pages 149 to 188. These are arranged under the headings of the various parts of speech : Nouns, Adjectives, Pronouns, etc. However, before an Exercise is attempted, the teacher should make certain that the students have comprehended the particular usage involved. An occasional reference to some specific Section may be made whenever this is deemed necessary, but under no circumstances is it advisable to go through the various Sections of the book consecutively, or to commit to memory rules concerning usage.

Despite the fact that this book has been designed for two separate uses, the writer is of the opinion that the best results will be achieved if it is used by the student both as a text-book and as a book of reference.

CHAPTER I

MISUSED FORMS

USING A WRONG PREPOSITION

Mistakes are often made by using a wrong preposition after certain words. The following list includes the words which most often give trouble:

1. Absorbed (= very much interested) **in,** not *at.*

· *Don't say:* The man was absorbed at his work.
Say: The man was **absorbed in** his work.

2. Accuse of, not *for.*

Don't say: He accused the man for stealing.
Say: He **accused** the man **of** stealing.

NOTE. But **"charge"** takes **"with"**: as, "The man was **charged with** murder."

3. Accustomed to, not *with.*

Don't say: I am accustomed with hot weather.
Say: I am **accustomed to** hot weather.

NOTE. Also **"used to"**: as, "He is **used to** the heat."

4. Afraid of, not *from.*

Don't say: The girl is afraid from the dog.
Say: The girl is **afraid of** the dog.

COMMON MISTAKES IN ENGLISH

5. Aim at, not *on* or *against*.

Don't say: He aimed on (*or* against) the bird.
Say: He **aimed at** the bird.

NOTE. The preposition **at** is often used to denote direction: as, **"throw at," "shout at," "fire at," "shoot at."** But **"shoot"** (without the **at**) means to kill: as, "He **shot** a bird" (= he hit and killed it).

6. Angry with, not *against*.

Don't say: The teacher was angry against him.
Say: The teacher was **angry with** him.

NOTE 1. We get **angry "with"** a person, but **"at"** a thing: as, "He was **angry at** the weather" (not: **"with the weather"**).
NOTE 2. Also **"annoyed with", "vexed with," "indignant with"** a person, but **"at"** a thing.

7. Anxious (= troubled) **about,** not *for*.

Don't say: They are anxious for his health.
Say: They are **anxious about** his health.

NOTE. But **"anxious"** meaning **"wishing very much"** takes **"for"**: as, "Parents are **anxious for** their children's success."

8. Arrive at, not *to*.

Don't say: We arrived to the village at night.
Say: We **arrived at** the village at night.

NOTE. **"Arrive in"** is used of countries and large cities: as, "Mr. Smith has **arrived in** London (New York, India, etc.)"

9. Ashamed of, not *from*.

Don't say: He is now ashamed from his conduct.
Say: He is now **ashamed of** his conduct.

NOTE. It is not proper to use **"ashamed of"** in the meaning of **"shy."** Thus, instead of "I am ashamed of my teacher," you should say, "I am **shy of** my teacher."

MISUSED FORMS

10. Believe in, not *to.*

Don't say: Christians believe to Jesus Christ.
Say: Christians **believe in** Jesus Christ.

NOTE. **"To believe in"** means to have faith in; while **"to believe"** (without the **in**) means to regard as true: as, "I quite believe what he says."

11. Benefit by, not *from.*

Don't say: She has benefited from the change.
Say: She has **benefited by** the change.

NOTE. But a person **gets** or **derives benefit from**: as, "She **got** (or **derived**) much **benefit from** the change."

12. Boast of or **about,** not *for.*

Don't say: He boasted for his riches.
Say: He **boasted of** (or **about**) his riches.

13. Careful of, not *for.*

Don't say: He is very careful for his health.
Say: He is very **careful of** his health.

NOTE. Also **"take care of"**: as, "He **takes care of** his money."

14. Come or **go by train,** etc., not *with the train,* etc.

Don't say: He came with the train yesterday.
Say: He **came by train** yesterday.

NOTE. We say: **"by train," "by tram," "by boat," "by aeroplane"**; also, **"by land," "by sea," "by air"; "by bus," "in a bus"** or **"on a bus"; "by motor-car"** or **"in a motor-car," "by taxi"** or **"in a taxi"; "in a cab," "in a carriage"; "on horseback," "on a donkey," "on a bicycle"; "on foot."**

15. Complain of, not *for.*

Don't say: Many people complain for the heat.
Say: Many people **complain of** the heat.

16. Composed of, not *from*.

> *Don't say:* Our class is composed from thirty boys.
> *Say:* Our class is **composed of** thirty boys.

17. Confidence in, not *to*.

> *Don't say:* I have great confidence to him.
> *Say:* I have great **confidence in** him.

NOTE. Also **"in confidence"**: as, "Let me tell you something **in confidence"** (= as a secret).

18. Conform to, not *with*.

> *Don't say:* We must conform with the rules.
> *Say:* We must **conform to** the rules.

NOTE. But **"comply"** takes **"with"**: as, "We will **comply with** your request."

19. Congratulate on, not *for*.

> *Don't say:* I congratulate you for your success.
> *Say:* I **congratulate** you **on** your success.

20. Consist of, not *from*.

> *Don't say:* A year consists from twelve months.
> *Say:* A year **consists of** twelve months.

NOTE. Great care must be taken never to use **"consist"** in the passive voice.

21. Covered with, not *by*.

> *Don't say:* The mountains are covered by snow.
> *Say:* The mountains are **covered with** snow.

22. Cure of, not *from*.

> *Don't say:* The man was cured from his illness.
> *Say:* The man was **cured of** his illness.

NOTE. But the noun **"cure"** takes **"for"**: as, "There is no **cure for** that disease."

MISUSED FORMS

23. Depend on or **upon**, not *from*.

> *Don't say:* It depends from himself.
> *Say:* It **depends on** (or **upon**) himself.

NOTE. Also **"rely on"** or **"upon"**: as, "I cannot **rely on** (or **upon**) him."

24. Deprive of, not *from*.

> *Don't say:* He was deprived from his freedom.
> *Say:* He was **deprived of** his freedom.

25. Die of an illness, not *from an illness*.

> *Don't say:* Many people have died from malaria.
> *Say:* Many people have **died of** malaria.

NOTE. Men **"die of illness," "of hunger," "of thirst," "of"** or **"from wounds"; "from overwork"; "by violence," "by the sword," "by pestilence"; "in battle," "in poverty"; "for their country," "for a cause"; "through neglect"; "on the scaffold"; "at the stake."**

26. Different from, not *than*.

> *Don't say:* My book is different than yours.
> *Say:* My book is **different from** yours.

27. Disappointed in, not *from*.

> *Don't say:* I was disappointed from his work.
> *Say:* I was **disappointed in** his work.

NOTE. We are **disappointed in** a thing when we see that it is not what we expected or desired, but we are **disappointed of** a thing when we fail to get it: as, "We were **disappointed of** our hopes."

28. Divide into parts, not *in parts*.

> *Don't say:* I divided the cake in four parts.
> *Say:* I **divided** the cake **into** four parts.

NOTE. But a thing may be divided **"in half"** or **"in two"**: as, "He **divided** the apple **in half** (or **in two**)."

29. Doubt (n.) **of** or **about,** not *for.*

> *Don't say:* I have no doubt for his ability.
> *Say:* I have no **doubt of** (or **about**) his ability.

NOTE. Also **"doubtful of"**: as, "I am **doubtful of** his ability to pass."

30. Dressed in, not *with.*

> *Don't say:* The woman was dressed with black.
> *Say:* The woman was **dressed in** black.

NOTE. "The woman was **in** black," is also correct.

31. Exception to, not *of.*

> *Don't say:* This is an exception of the rule.
> *Say:* This is an **exception to** the rule.

NOTE. But we say **"with the exception of"**: as, "He liked all his studies **with the exception of** Latin."

32. Exchange for, not *by.*

> *Don't say:* They exchanged wheat by machinery.
> *Say:* They **exchanged** wheat **for** machinery.

NOTE. Also **"in exchange for"**: as, "He gave his old car **in exchange for** a new one."

33. Fail in, not *from.*

> *Don't say:* He failed from mathematics last year.
> *Say:* He **failed in** mathematics last year.

34. Full of, not *with* or *from.*

> *Don't say:* The jar was full with (*or* from) oil.
> *Say:* The jar was **full of** oil.

NOTE. But **"fill"** takes **"with"**: as, "He **filled** the glass **with** water."

35. Get rid of, not *from.*

> *Don't say:* I shall be glad to get rid from him.
> *Say:* I shall be glad to **get rid of** him.

MISUSED FORMS

36. Glad of or **about,** not *from* or *with*.

Don't say: I am glad from (*or* with) the news.
Say: I am **glad of** (or **about**) the news.

NOTE. But a person is **"glad at"** a result: as, "He is **glad at** having received a good mark."

37. Good at, not *in*.

Don't say: My brother is good in mathematics.
Say: My brother is **good at** mathematics.

NOTE 1. Also **"bad at," "clever at," "quick at," "slow at,"** etc. But **"weak in"**: as, "He is **weak in** grammar."
NOTE 2. "He is **good in** class" means that his conduct is good.

38. Guard against, not *from*.

Don't say: You must guard from bad habits.
Say: You must **guard against** bad habits.

39. Guilty of, not *for*.

Don't say: He was found guilty for murder.
Say: He was found **guilty of** murder.

40. Independent of, not *from*.

Don't say: He is independent from his parents.
Say: He is **independent of** his parents.

NOTE. But we say **"dependent on"**: as, "A child is **dependent on** its parents."

41. Indifferent to, not *for*.

Don't say: They are indifferent for politics.
Say: They are **indifferent to** politics.

42. Insist on, not *to*.

Don't say: He always insisted to his opinion.
Say: He always **insisted on** his opinion.

NOTE. But **"persist"** takes **"in"**: as, "He **persisted in** his foolish ideas."

COMMON MISTAKES IN ENGLISH

43. Interested in, not *for*.

> *Don't say:* She is not interested for her work.
> *Say:* She is not **interested in** her work.

NOTE. Also **"take an interest in"**: as, "She takes a great interest in music."

44. Jealous of, not *from*.

> *Don't say:* He is very jealous from his brother.
> *Say:* He is very **jealous of** his brother.

45. Leave for a place, not *to a place*.

> *Don't say:* They are leaving to England soon.
> *Say:* They are **leaving for** England soon.

46. Live on, not *from*.

> *Don't say:* He lives from his brother's money.
> *Say:* He **lives on** his brother's money.

NOTE. Also **"feed on"**: as, "Some birds **feed on** insects."

47. Look at, not *to*.

> *Don't say:* Look to this beautiful picture.
> *Say:* **Look at** this beautiful picture.

NOTE. Also **"gaze at," "stare at,"** etc. But: **"look after"** (= take care of); **"look for"** (= try to find); **"look over"** (= examine); **"look into"** (= examine closely); **"look upon"** (= consider); **"look down upon"** (= have a low opinion of); **"look up to"** (= respect); **"look out for"** (= expect); **"look forward to"** (= expect with pleasure); **"look to"** (= be careful of *or* rely on).

48. Married to, not *with*.

> *Don't say:* She was married with a rich man.
> *Say:* She was **married to** a rich man.

NOTE. Also **"engaged to"**: as, "Miss Jones was **engaged to** Mr. Smith."

MISUSED FORMS

49. Opposite to, not *from.*

> *Don't say:* Their house is opposite from ours.
> *Say:* Their house is **opposite to** ours.

50. Pass by a place, not *from a place.*

> *Don't say:* Will you pass from the post-office?
> *Say:* Will you **pass by** the post-office?

51. Play for a team, not *with a team.*

> *Don't say:* He plays regularly with that team.
> *Say:* He **plays** regularly **for** that team.

52. Pleased with, not *from.*

> *Don't say:* The teacher is pleased from me.
> *Say:* The teacher is **pleased with** me.

NOTE. But we may say **"pleased at"** or **"pleased with"** if an abstract noun or a clause follows: as, "They were **pleased at** (or **with**) what he said"; "They were **pleased at** (or **with**) his gentleness."

53. Popular with, not *among.*

> *Don't say:* John is popular among his friends.
> *Say:* John is **popular with** his friends.

54. Prefer to, not *from.*

> *Don't say:* I prefer a blue pen from a red one.
> *Say:* I **prefer** a blue pen **to** a red one.

NOTE. Also **"preferable to"**: as, "Work is **preferable to** idleness."

55. Preside at or **over,** not *in.*

> *Don't say:* Who presided in the last meeting?
> *Say:* Who **presided at** (or **over**) the last meeting?

COMMON MISTAKES IN ENGLISH

56. Proud of, not *for*.

Don't say: He is very proud for his promotion.
Say: He is very **proud of** his promotion.

NOTE. But we say **"take (a) pride in"**: as, "A craftsman **takes a pride in** his work."

57. Rejoice at or in, not *for*.

Don't say: We rejoiced for his success.
Say: We **rejoiced at** (or **in**) his success.

58. Related to, not *with*.

Don't say: Are you related with him in any way?
Say: Are you **related to** him in any way?

NOTE. Also **"relation to"**: as, "Is he any **relation to** you?"

59. Repent of, not *from*.

Don't say: He repented from his wrongdoing.
Say: He **repented of** his wrongdoing.

NOTE. But **"repentance"** takes **"for"**: as, "He feels **repentance for** his sin."

60. Satisfied with, not *from*.

Don't say: Are you satisfied from your marks?
*Say***:** Are you **satisfied with** your marks?

NOTE. Also **"content with," "delighted with"**; **"displeased with," "dissatisfied with," "disgusted with."**

61. Similar to, not *with*.

Don't say: Your book is not similar with mine.
Say: Your book is not **similar to** mine.

62. Sit at a desk, etc., not *on a desk*, etc.

Don't say: The teacher often sits on his desk.

Say: The teacher often **sits at his desk.**

NOTE. Also "sit at a table." But: "on a chair," "on a bench," "on a sofa," etc.; "in an arm-chair," "in a tree" or "up a tree." "A bird sometimes **perches** (= sits) **on** a tree."

63. Spend on, not *for.*

Don't say: I spend a lot of time for my stamps.
Say: I **spend** a lot of time **on** my stamps.

64. Succeed in, not *at.*

Don't say: I hope he will succeed at his work.
Say: I hope he will **succeed in** his work.

NOTE. But a person **succeeds to** a property, a title, or an office: as, "Queen Elizabeth II **succeeded to** the throne in 1952."

65. Superior to, not *from* or *than.*

Don't say: This is superior from (*or* than) that.
Say: This is **superior to** that.

NOTE. Also "inferior to," "junior to," "senior to," "prior to."

66. Sure of, not *for.*

Don't say: I am quite sure for his honesty.
Say: I am quite **sure of** his honesty.

NOTE. Also "certain of": as, "I am quite **certain of** it."

67. Surprised at, not *for.*

Don't say: We were surprised for his failure.
Say: We were **surprised at** his failure.

NOTE. Also "astonished at," "amazed at," "alarmed at," "puzzled at," "shocked at."

68. Suspect of, not *for.*

Don't say: I suspect him for stealing the pen.
Say: I **suspect** him **of** stealing the pen.

NOTE. Also "suspicious of": as, "Dogs are **suspicious of** strangers."

69. Take by, not *from*.

Don't say: He took his brother from the hand.
Say: He **took** his brother **by** the hand.

NOTE. Also **"hold by," "catch by," "seize by," "snatch by," "grasp by."**

70. Tie to, not *on*.

Don't say: The man tied the horse on a tree.
Say: The man **tied** the horse **to** a tree.

NOTE. Also **"bind to"**: as, "The prisoner was **bound to** the stake."

71. Tired of, not *from*.

Don't say: The boys are tired from boiled eggs.
Say: The boys are **tired of** boiled eggs.

NOTE. **"Tired with"** means with no energy or strength left: as, "I am **tired with** walking; I want to rest." So also **"weary of"** and **"weary with."**

72. Translate into, not *to*.

Don't say: Translate this passage to English.
Say: **Translate** this passage **into** English.

73. Tremble with cold, etc., not *from cold*, etc.

Don't say: The man was trembling from cold.
Say: The man was **trembling with** cold.

NOTE. Also **"shake with"** and **"shiver with"**: as, "The thief was **shaking with** fear."

74. Warn (a person) **of danger,** not *about danger*.

Don't say: They were warned about the danger.
Say: They were **warned of** the danger.

NOTE. But we **warn** a person **against** a fault: as, "His teacher **warned** him **against** disobeying the regulations."

MISUSED FORMS

75. Write in ink, not *with ink.*

> *Don't say:* I have written the letter with ink.
> *Say:* I have **written** the letter **in ink.**

NOTE. To "**write in** ink," "**in** pencil," or "**in** chalk" means the marks that a pen, a pencil, or a piece of chalk makes. If, however, the instrument is meant by which the writing is done, we use "**with**" instead of "**in**": as, "**I write with** (a pen, a pencil, or a piece of chalk)."

(See Exercises 76–79 on pages 176–178.)

(See Exercises 76–79 on pages 176–178.)

MISUSE OF THE INFINITIVE

The gerund and not the infinitive should be used:

(*a*) After prepositions or preposition phrases:

76. Without, etc. + **-ing.**

> *Don't say:* Do your work without to speak.
> *Say:* Do your work **without speaking.**

77. Instead of, etc. + **-ing.**

> *Don't say:* He went away instead to wait.
> *Say:* He went away **instead of waiting.**

(*b*) After words which regularly take a preposition:

78. Capable of + **-ing.**

> *Don't say:* He is quite capable to do that.
> *Say:* He is quite **capable of doing** that.

NOTE. Also "**incapable of**"; but "**able**" or "**unable**" is followed by the infinitive: as, "He is **unable to do** anything."

79. Fond of + **-ing.**

> *Don't say:* She is always fond to talk.
> *Say:* She is always **fond of talking.**

Have another look at—

PREPOSITIONS AFTER CERTAIN WORDS

Note carefully the prepositions used after the following words:

accuse *of*	good *at*
accustomed *to*	guard *against*
afraid *of*	guilty *of*
aim *at*	independent *of*
angry *with, at*	indifferent *to*
arrive *at, in*	insist *on*
ashamed *of*	interested *in*
believe *in*	jealous *of*
benefit *by*	look *at*
boast *of*	married *to*
careful *of*	pleased *with*
complain *of*	prefer *to*
composed *of*	proud *of*
conform *to*	related *to*
congratulate *on*	repent *of*
consist *of*	satisfied *with*
cure *of*	similar *to*
depend *on*	succeed *in*
deprive *of*	superior *to*
die *of*	sure *of*
different *from*	surprised *at*
doubt *of* or *about*	suspect *of*
dressed *in*	tired *with, of*
fail *in*	translate *into*
full *of*	warn *of*

MISUSED FORMS

80. Insist on + -ing.

> *Don't say:* He insisted to go to London.
> *Say:* He **insisted on going** to London.

81. Object to + -ing.

> *Don't say:* I object to be treated like this.
> *Say:* I **object to being** treated like this.

82. Prevent from + -ing.

> *Don't say:* The rain prevented me to go.
> *Say:* The rain **prevented me from going.**

83. Succeed in + -ing.

> *Don't say:* He succeeded to gain the prize.
> *Say:* He **succeeded in gaining** the prize.

84. Think of + -ing.

> *Don't say:* I often think to go to England.
> *Say:* I often **think of going** to England.

85. Tired of + -ing.

> *Don't say:* The customer grew tired to wait.
> *Say:* The customer grew **tired of waiting.**

86. Used to + -ing.

> *Don't say:* She is used to get up early.
> *Say:* She is **used to getting** up early.

(*c*) After certain verbs:

87. Avoid + -ing.

> *Don't say:* You can't avoid to make mistakes.
> *Say:* You can't **avoid making** mistakes.

NOTE. Also "**can't help**" (= can't avoid): as, "**I can't help laughing.**"

COMMON MISTAKES IN ENGLISH

88. Enjoy + -ing.

Don't say: I enjoy to play a game of football.
   Say: I **enjoy playing** a game of football.

NOTE. Verbs meaning **"to like"** or **"to dislike"** may be followed either by the infinitive or the gerund: as, "He **likes reading** English books," *or* "He **likes to read** English books."

89. Excuse + -ing.

Don't say: Please excuse me to be so late.
   Say: Please **excuse my being** so late.
   Or: Please **excuse me for being** so late.

90. Finish + -ing.

Don't say: Have you not finished to speak?
   Say: Have you not **finished speaking**?

NOTE. Verbs meaning **"to begin"** are followed either by the gerund or the infinitive: as, "She **began to speak**," *or* "She **began speaking**."

91. Go on (continue) + -ing.

Don't say: The music went on to play all day.
   Say: The music **went on playing** all day.

NOTE. Also **"keep on"**: as, "She **kept on playing** the piano."

92. Mind (object to) + -ing.

Don't say: Would you mind to open the door?
   Say: Would you **mind opening** the door?

93. Practise + -ing.

Don't say: You must practise to speak English.
   Say: You must **practise speaking** English.

94. Remember + -ing.

Don't say: I do not remember to have seen him.

Say: I do not **remember seeing** him.

Or: I do not **remember having** seen him.

95. Risk + -ing.

Don't say: We couldn't risk to leave him alone.

Say: We couldn't **risk leaving** him alone.

96. Stop + -ing.

Don't say: The wind has almost stopped to blow.

Say: The wind has almost **stopped blowing.**

NOTE. Also "give up" (= stop): as, "He gave up smoking."

(*d*) After certain adjectives:

97. Busy + -ing.

Don't say: He was busy to prepare his lessons.

Say: He was **busy preparing** his lessons.

98. Worth + -ing.

Don't say: Is today's film worth to see?

Say: Is today's film **worth seeing**?

(*e*) After certain phrases:

99. Have difficulty in + -ing.

Don't say: He has no difficulty to do it.

Say: He has no **difficulty in doing** it.

100. Have the pleasure of + -ing.

Don't say: I had the pleasure to meet him.

Say: **I had the pleasure of meeting** him.

NOTE. Also "take pleasure in": as, "He takes great pleasure in helping the poor."

COMMON MISTAKES IN ENGLISH

101. It's no use + -ing.

Don't say: It's no use to cry like a baby.
Say: **It's no use crying** like a baby.

102. It's no good + -ing.

Don't say: It's no good to get angry at once.
Say: **It's no good getting** angry at once.

103. Look forward to + -ing.

Don't say: I look forward to see him soon.
Say: I **look forward to seeing** him soon.

104. There is no harm in + -ing.

Don't say: There's no harm to visit him now.
Say: **There's no harm in visiting** him now.

(See Exercises 65 and 66 on page 172.)

THE USE OF A WRONG TENSE

105. Using the past tense after **"did"** instead of the infinitive without **"to."**

(*a*) To ask questions:

Don't say: Did you went to school yesterday?
Say: **Did** you **go** to school yesterday?

(*b*) To make negations:

Don't say: I did not went to school yesterday.
Say: I **did** not **go** to school yesterday.

After the auxiliary **"did"** the present infinitive without **"to"** must be used, and not the past tense of the indicative.

NOTE. The answer to a question beginning with **"Did"** is always in the past tense: as, "**Did** you see the picture?"—"Yes, I **saw** the picture"; *or* "Yes, I **did**."

Have another look at—

THE USE OF THE GERUND

The gerund (and not the infinitive) should be used:

(1) After prepositions.

EXAMPLES: He worked *without stopping*. She played *instead of working*.

(2) After words which regularly take a preposition, such as *fond of, insist on, tired of, succeed in*.

EXAMPLES: I am *tired of doing* the work again. He *succeeded in killing* the tiger.

(3) After certain verbs, such as *avoid, enjoy, finish, stop, risk, excuse*.

EXAMPLES: Boys *enjoy playing* football. The wind has *stopped blowing*.

(4) After the adjectives *busy* and *worth*.

EXAMPLES: He was *busy writing* a book. This date is *worth remembering*.

(5) After certain phrases, such as *it's no use, it's no good, I can't help, would you mind, look forward to*.

EXAMPLES: I think *it's no use trying* again. *I can't help feeling* angry about it.

The gerund or the infinitive can be used after certain verbs, such as *begin, like, dislike, hate, love, prefer*.

EXAMPLE: He began to talk *or* He began talking.

106. Using the third person singular after **"does"** instead of the infinitive without **"to."**

(*a*) To ask questions:

Don't say: Does the gardener waters the flowers?
    Say: **Does** the gardener **water** the flowers?

(*b*) To make negations:

Don't say: The man does not waters the flowers.
    Say: The man **does not water** the flowers.

After the auxiliary **"does"** the present infinitive without **"to"** must be used, and not the third person of the present indicative.

NOTE. The answer to a question beginning with **"Does"** is always in the present tense, third person: as, **"Does** he like the cinema?"—"Yes, he **likes** the cinema"; *or* "Yes, he **does**."

(For §§ 105–106 see Exercises 34 and 35 on page 162.)

107. Using the third person singular after **"can," "must,"** etc., instead of the infinitive without **"to."**

Don't say: He can speaks English very well.
    Say: He **can speak** English very well.

After the verbs **"can," "must," "may," "shall,"** and **"will,"** the present infinitive without **"to"** must be used, and not the third person of the present indicative.

108. Wrong sequence of tenses.

Don't say: He asked me what I am doing.
    Say: He **asked** me what I **was** doing.

When the verb in the principal clause is in the past tense, only a past tense can be used in subordinate clauses.

NOTE. But this rule does not apply (1) to verbs within quotations, (2) to facts that are true at all times, and (3) to comparisons. Thus we say:
    1. He **said**, "I **am** waiting for your answer."
    2. He **said** that London **is** a great city.
    3. He **liked** you more than he **likes** me.

MISUSED FORMS

109. Using *"shall"* or *"will"* instead of **"should"** or **"would"** in a subordinate clause.

Don't say: He said that he will come tomorrow.
Say: He **said** that he **would** come tomorrow.

"Shall" and "will" change to "should" and "would" in subordinate clauses, when the verb in the principal clause is in a past tense.

110. Using *"may"* instead of **"might"** in a subordinate clause.

Don't say: He told me that he may come today.
Say: He **told** me that he **might** come today.

"May" changes to "might" in subordinate clauses, when the verb in the principal clause is in the past tense.

NOTE. The conjunction **"that"** is never preceded by a comma.

111. Using *"can"* instead of **"could"** in a subordinate clause.

Don't say: He thought he can win the prize.
Say: He **thought** he **could** win the prize.

"Can" changes to "could" in subordinate clauses, when the verb in the principal clause is in the past tense.

(For §§ 108–111 see Exercises 23 and 24 on page 158.)

112. Using the past tense after the sign of the infinitive **"to."**

Don't say: He tried to kicked the ball away.
Say: He tried **to kick** the ball away.

The past tense of the indicative mood cannot be used after the infinitive sign **"to."**

113. Using the past tense after an auxiliary verb, instead of the past participle.

Don't say: I have forgot to bring my book.

Say: I **have forgotten** to bring my book.

The past participle (and not the past tense) should be used with the auxiliary verb "have" and its parts.

114. Using *"must"* or *"ought"* to express a past obligation.

Don't say: You ought to come yesterday.

Say: { You ought **to have come** yesterday.
You **should have come** yesterday; *or*
You **had to** come yesterday.

"Must" and **"ought"** cannot be used as past tenses. To express a past duty (which was not done) we may use the perfect infinitive after **"ought"** or **"should,"** or such expressions as **"had to," "was obliged to."**

NOTE. But in indirect speech **"must"** and **"ought"** may be used as past tenses: as, "He **said** he **must** do it."

115. Using the present perfect instead of the past tense.

Don't say: I have seen a good film yesterday.

Say: I **saw** a good film **yesterday**.

The past tense (and not the present perfect) should be used for an action completed in the past at a stated time.

NOTE. When your sentence has a word or a phrase denoting past time, like **"yesterday," "last night," "last week," "last year," "then," "ago,"** etc., be sure always to use a past tense.

116. Using the past tense instead of the present perfect.

Don't say: I saw the Parthenon of Athens.

Say: I **have seen** the Parthenon of Athens.

If we are speaking of the result of a past action rather than of the action itself, we must use the present perfect tense. When somebody says, "I **have seen** the Parthenon" he is not thinking so much of the past act of seeing it, as of the present result of that past action.

117. Using the past tense with a recent action, instead of the present perfect.

22

Don't say: The clock struck.
Say: The clock **has struck.**

If we are speaking of an action just finished, we must use the present perfect instead of the past tense. For instance, immediately after the clock strikes, we should not say "The clock struck," but "The clock **has struck.**"

118. Using the simple present instead of the present perfect.

Don't say: I am in this school two years.
Say: I **have been** in this school two years.

The present perfect (and not the simple present) must be used for an action begun in the past and continuing into the present. "**I have been** in this school two years" means **I am still here.**

119. Using the simple present instead of the present perfect in the answer to a **"since"** clause of time.

Don't say: Since he came, we are happy.
Say: Since he came, we **have been** happy.

The verb in the answer to a **"since"** clause of time is generally in the present perfect tense.

120. Using the simple present instead of the present continuous.

Don't say: Look! Two boys fight.
Say: Look! Two boys **are fighting.**

The present continuous (and not the simple present) must be used for an action going on at the time of speaking.

NOTE. The present continuous is also used for actions in the near future, especially with verbs of motion such as **"come,"** **"go,"** **"leave,"** etc.: as, "He **is leaving** for England soon."

121. The continuous form of the tense misused.

Don't say: I am understanding the lesson now.
Say: I **understand** the lesson now.

As a rule, verbs denoting a state rather than an act have no continuous forms, like **"understand," "know," "believe," "like,"** **"love," "belong," "prefer," "consist," "mean," "hear," "see,"** etc.

122. Using the present continuous for a habitual action, instead of the simple present.

Don't say: Every morning I am going for a walk.
Say: Every morning I **go** for a walk.

The simple present (and not the present continuous) should be used to express a present habitual action.

NOTE. But the present continuous may express a habitual action when used with the word **"always"** or with a verb denoting a continuous state: as, **"He is always talking** in class"; **"He is living** in London."

123. Using the verb *"to use"* for a present habitual action.

Don't say: I use to rise at six every morning.
Say: **I rise** at six every morning.
Or: **I am accustomed to** rising at six, etc.

The verb **"to use"** does not express a habit in the present. "I use" means "I employ": as, "**I use** a fountain-pen to write with."

NOTE. But in the past tense the verb **"to use"** expresses a past habitual action, and it usually refers to some remote habit or one no longer followed: as, "**I used to** see him every day"; "My father **used to** play football very well."

124. Using the past continuous for a habitual action, instead of the simple past tense.

Don't say: Last year I was walking to school every day.
Say: Last year I **walked** to school every day.

A habit in the past is expressed by the simple past tense, and not by the past continuous.

NOTE. The past continuous tense is used to describe events in the past continuing at the time another action took place: as, "I **was walking** to school when I **met** him."

125. Using the past tense instead of the past perfect.

> *Don't say:* The train left before I arrived.
>> *Say:* The train **had left** before I arrived.

The past perfect should be used when the time of one past action is more past than that of another. The action which was completed first is put in the past perfect and the second action in the past tense.

NOTE. The present tense and the past perfect should never be used in the same sentence. Thus, it would be incorrect to say, "My brother **says** that he **had** not **gone** to the cinema last night."

126. Using the past perfect instead of the past tense.

> *Don't say:* I had finished the book yesterday.
>> *Say:* I **finished** the book yesterday.

The past perfect should not be used unless there is another verb in the past tense in the same sentence.

(See § 125.)

127. Using the future in a clause of time, instead of the present tense.

> *Don't say:* I shall see you when I shall come back.
>> *Say:* I shall see you **when I come** back.

If the verb in the principal clause is in the future, the verb in the time clause must be in the present tense.

128. Using the future in the **"if"** clause instead of the present tense.

> *Don't say:* If he will ask me, I shall stay.
>> *Say:* **If he asks** me, I shall stay.

In a simple future condition, the present tense is used in the condition (or "if" clause) and the future tense in the answer to the condition.

NOTE. But the future tense may be used in an **"if"** clause expressing a request: as, "I **shall be** very grateful if you **will** lend me some money."

129. Using the present tense after **"as if"** or **"as though"** instead of the past.

Don't say: He talks as if he knows everything.
Say: He talks **as if he knew** everything.

The phrase **"as if"** or **"as though"** should be followed by the past tense. "He talks as if he knew everything" means "He talks as **he would talk** if he knew everything."

NOTE. With the verb **"to be"** the subjunctive **"were"** is often used after **"as if"**: as, "He acts **as if he were** a rich man."

130. Using the past conditional of **"wish"** instead of the present indicative.

Don't say: I would wish to know more English.
Say: **I wish (that) I knew** more English.

To express a present meaning the present tense of **"wish"** is used, followed by a **"that"** clause containing a past tense.

131. Using a wrong tense with an **"improbable"** condition.

Don't say: If he would ask me, I should stay.
Say: **If he asked me, I should stay.**

An **"improbable"** condition is expressed by the past tense and answered by the conditional. This use of the past tense does not indicate a time but a degree of probability.

132. Using a wrong tense with an **"impossible"** condition.

Don't say: If he would have asked me, I should stay.
Say: **If he had asked me, I should have stayed.**

An **"impossible"** condition is expressed by the past perfect and answered by the past conditional. This use of the past perfect does not indicate a time but an impossible happening.

MISUSED FORMS

133. Using the infinitive instead of a finite verb.

> *Don't say:* Sir, to go home to bring my book?
> *Say:* Sir, **may I go** home to bring my book?

The infinitive simply names an action without reference to person, number or time. Therefore, it cannot make sense without the help of a finite verb.

134. Mixing up the tenses.

> *Don't say:* They asked him to be captain, but he refuses.
> *Say:* They **asked** him to be captain, but he **refused.**

If you begin with a verb referring to past time, keep the same form all through. The same rule applies to tenses throughout a composition.

(See Exercises 25–31 on pages 159–161.)

MISCELLANEOUS EXAMPLES

135. Confusion of gender.

> *Don't say:* The door is open: please shut her.
> *Say:* The door is open: please shut **it**.

In English only names of persons and animals have gender (masculine or feminine). Things without life are neuter, and take the pronoun "**it**" in the singular.

NOTE. But when things without life are personified, they take masculine or feminine pronouns: as, "**Time** has **his** work to do"; "**England** is proud of **her** navy."

136. Using the possessive form for things without life.

> *Don't say:* His room's window is open.
> *Say:* **The window of his room** is open.

The possessive form is used for persons and animals only. For things without life, which cannot possess, the objective with "**of**" should be used.

Have another look at—

THE USE OF CERTAIN TENSES

1. The Simple Present is used for habitual actions, while the Present Continuous is used for actions taking place at the present moment.

> EXAMPLES: I *read* the newspaper every day. I *am reading* English (now).

2. The Simple Past is used when a definite time or date is mentioned, while the Present Perfect is used when no time is mentioned.

> EXAMPLES: I *wrote* my exercise *last night*. I *have written* my exercise.

3. Habitual actions in the past are expressed either by the Simple Past or by the phrase *used to*.

> EXAMPLE: I *went* (or *I used to go*) to the cinema every week last year.

NOTE. The Past Continuous (*I was going*) is not used for a past habitual action, but for an action in the past continuing at the time another action took place: as, "I *was going* to the cinema when I met him."

4. If the action began in the past and is still continuing in the present, the only correct tense to use is the Present Perfect.

> EXAMPLE: I *have been* in this class for two months.

5. Be very careful NOT to use the future but the Present tense in a clause of time or condition, if the verb in the principal clause is in the future.

> EXAMPLE: I shall visit the Parthenon *when I go* (or *if I go*) to Athens.

MISUSED FORMS

NOTE. But we say: "a day's work," " a night's rest," "a week's holiday," "a shilling's worth," "the sun's rays," "the court's decision," "a boat's crew," "London's population," etc.

137. Using the objective case after the verb **"to be."**

Don't say: It was him.
Say: It was **he.**

The pronoun coming after the verb **"to be"** must be in the nominative case, and not in the objective.

NOTE. The common expression "It's **me**" is strictly an error, yet it is the accepted form in conversation. "It is **I**" remains the correct form in written composition.

138. Using the objective case after the conjunction **"than."**

Don't say: My brother is taller than me.
Say: My brother is taller **than I (am).**

The word **"than"** is a conjunction, and can only be followed by a pronoun in the nominative case. The verb coming after the pronoun is generally omitted.

NOTE. In spoken English the objective case is often used: as, "You're much taller **than me.**"

139. Using the nominative case after **"between."**

Don't say: It is a secret between you and I.
Say: It is a secret **between** you and **me.**

"Between" is a preposition, and all prepositions take the objective case after them.

140. Using the objective case before a gerund.

Don't say: There is no use in me learning it.
Say: There is no use in **my** learning it.

When a word ending in **"-ing"** is used as a gerund, any noun or pronoun coming before it must be in the possessive case.

141. Using the objective case with the double possessive.

Don't say: A friend of him told us the news.

29

Say: **A friend of his** told us the news.

The double possessive (**of** + **mine, yours, his,** etc.) is often used when we wish to emphasize the person who possesses rather than the thing which he possesses. "**A friend of his**" is simply another way of saying "**one of his friends.**"

142. Misuse of "**-self**" forms.

Don't say: George and myself are present.
Say: George and **I** are present.

The simple personal pronouns **I, you, he,** etc., should be used, if no emphasis is necessary.

NOTE. The "**-self**" pronouns are used in two ways: (1) for emphasis: as, "She **herself** was hurt"; (2) reflexively: as, "She hurt **herself.**"

143. Using "*hisself*" or "*theirselves*" instead of "**himself**" or "**themselves.**"

Don't say: They fell down and hurt theirselves.
Say: They fell down and hurt **themselves.**

The reflexive pronouns, third person, are "**himself**" and "**themselves,**" and not "hisself" and "theirselves."

144. The cognate object misused.

Don't say: Michael played a very good play.
Say: Michael **played** a very good **game.**

In English the use of a cognate object—an object having the same form and meaning as the verb—is not common, but is restricted to only a few expressions: as, "**to sing a fine song,**" "**to fight a good fight,**" "**to dream a strange dream,**" "**to live a long life,**" "**to die a sad death.**"

145. Using the relative pronoun "*which*" for persons.

Don't say: I have a brother which is at school.
Say: I have a brother **who** is at school.

"**Which,**" as a relative pronoun, is to be used only for animals or things. The right pronoun to use for persons is "**who (whose, whom).**"

MISUSED FORMS

146. Using *"which"* or *"what"* after **"all,"** etc.

Don't say: I know all which (*or* what) he said.
Say: I know **all (that)** he said.

The relative pronouns **"which"** and **"what"** cannot be used after **"all," "some," "any," "something," "everything," "anything," "much," "little"** and **"nothing."** Only the relative **"that"** may be used after these words, but it is commonly omitted.

147. Who and **whom.**

(*a*) Who.

Don't say: I saw the man whom you said was away.
Say: I saw the man **who** you said **was** away.

(*b*) Whom.

Don't say: He is a man who I know you can trust.
Say: He is a man **whom** I know **you can trust.**

In sentence (*a*) **"who"** is the subject of **"was"**; "you said" is a mere parenthesis. In sentence (*b*) **"whom"** is the object of **"you can trust"**; "I know" is a mere parenthesis.

(For §§ 145–147 see Exercise 19 on page 156.)

148. Using *"who," "whom,"* or *"which"* after the superlative, instead of **"that."**

Don't say: It is the best which I have seen.
Say: It is **the best (that)** I have seen.

The relative **"that"** (not **"who," "whom,"** or **"which"**) should be used after a superlative. It can, however, be omitted.

149. Using a wrong relative after **"same"** or **"such."**

Don't say: He wears the same coat that I wear.
Say: He wears the **same** coat **as** I wear.

After **"same"** and **"such"** the relative **"as"** should be used.

NOTE. But **"that"** (not **"who"** or **"which"**) can sometimes be used after **"same"**: as, "He wore the **same** clothes **that** he wore on Sunday."

150. Using *"who?"* or *"what?"* instead of **"which?"**

Don't say: Who of the two boys is the taller?
Say: **Which** of the two boys is the taller?

The interrogative pronoun **"Which?"** is used for both persons and things, and asks for **one** out of a definite number.

NOTE. The interrogative pronoun **"what?"** does not imply choice: as, **"What** is your telephone number?" It is also used to ask for a person's profession: as, **"What** is your father?"— "He is a lawyer."

(Compare § 145.)

151. Who? and **Whom?**

(*a*) Who?

Don't say: Whom do you think will be chosen?
Say: **Who** do you think **will be chosen?**

(*b*) Whom?

Don't say: Who do you think I saw yesterday?
Say: **Whom** do you think **I saw** yesterday?

In sentence (*a*) **"who"** is the subject of **"will be chosen"**; "do you think" is a mere parenthesis. In sentence (*b*) **"whom"** is the object of **"I saw"**; "do you think" is a mere parenthesis.

(For §§ 150 and 151 see Exercise 20 on page 156.)

152. Using *"his"* as an indefinite pronoun.

Don't say: One should take care of his health.
Say: **One** should take care of **one's** health.

The indefinite pronoun **"one"** must be followed by one of its parts (**one, one's, oneself**), and not by **he, she, it**, or their parts.

NOTE. It is, however, advisable to avoid using **"one"** as subject, and to use instead such words as **"boy," "girl," "man"**: as, "A **boy** should take care of **his** health."

MISUSED FORMS

153. Each other and **One another.**

(*a*) Each other.

Don't say: These two boys help one another.
Say: These **two** boys help **each other**.

(*b*) One another.

Don't say: These three boys help each other.
Say: These **three** boys help **one another**.

"Each other" is better used when there are two people concerned, and **"one another"** when there are more than two people concerned. Many writers, however, do not observe this distinction.

154. Using "*one other*" instead of **"another."**

Don't say: Please give me one other book.
Say: Please give me **another** book.

"Another" is formed from "an" and "other", but instead of being written **"an other"** or **"one other,"** they are written as one word **"another."**

155. Using the superlative instead of the comparative.

Don't say: John is the tallest of the two boys.
Say: John is the **taller** of the **two** boys.

When two persons or things are compared, the comparative must be used.

156. Using "*from*" after the comparative instead of **"than."**

Don't say: John is taller from his brother.
Say: John is **taller than** his brother.

Adjectives (or adverbs) in the comparative are followed by **"than"** and not by **"from."**

157. Using the comparative instead of the superlative.

Don't say: Cairo is the larger city in Africa.

Say: Cairo is the **largest** city in **Africa.**

When **more than two** persons or things are compared, the superlative must be used.

158. Using *"the more"* instead of **"most."**

Don't say: The more people will agree with me.
Say: **Most** people will agree with me.

"Most" (not "the more") should be used when we mean "the majority of."

159. Using *"more good"* or *"more bad"* instead of **"better"** or **"worse."**

Don't say: This one looks more good than that. .
Say: This one looks **better** than that.

The adjectives **"good"** and **"bad"** have irregular forms of comparison: **"good, better, best"** and **"bad, worse, worst."**

(For §§ 155–159 see Exercises 8 and 9 on pages 151–152.)

160. Using *"home"* instead of **"at home."**

Don't say: In the afternoon I stay home.
Say: In the afternoon I stay **at home.**

The phrase **"at home"** should be used to mean "in the house." But with such verbs as **"come"** or **"go"** no preposition is necessary: as, "He wants to go **home.**"

161. Using *"from"* instead of **"one of"** or **"among."**

Don't say: She is from the best girls I know.
Say: She is **one of the best** girls I know.

You should avoid using "from" in the sense of **"one of"** or **"among."**

162. Using the passive infinitive instead of the active.

Don't say: English is not easy to be learnt.

Say: English is not easy **to learn.**

The adjectives **"easy," "difficult," "hard," "heavy," "good,"** etc., are generally followed by the active infinitive.

163. Using an intransitive verb in the passive voice.

Don't say: She was disappeared from the house.
Say: She **disappeared** from the house.

As a rule, intransitive verbs, like **appear, seem, become, consist,** cannot be used in the passive voice.

164. Mixing up one form of the verb with another.

Don't say: It is better to do some work well while young than spending all the time in play.
Say: It is better **to do** some work well while young than **to spend** all the time in play.

Care should be taken that one form of the verb is not mixed with another: if the first verb in a comparison is in the infinitive mood, the second must also be in the infinitive.

165. Wrong sequence of moods.

Don't say: If you would do me this favour, I shall be very grateful to you.
Say: **If you would** do me this favour, **I should** be very grateful to you.
Or: **If you will** do me this favour, **I shall** be very grateful to you.

In a conditional sentence either both verbs must be in the subjunctive mood or both in the indicative.

166. The unrelated participle.

Don't say: Being in haste, the door was left open.
Say: **Being in haste, he** left the door open.

Care must be taken to provide the logical subject relating to the

35

participial phrase. In the sentence given, the logical subject to **"being in haste"** is, of course, **"he"** and not "the **door**."

167. The question phrase *"isn't it?"* misused.

Don't say: He played well yesterday, isn't it?
Say: He played well yesterday, **didn't he**?

The question phrase **"isn't it"** is used only when the preceding statement contains the word **"is"**: as, " It **is** a hot day, **isn't it?**"

NOTE. In this form of question, the same tense and person must be used as in the preceding statement and the correct auxiliary must be used. If, however, the preceding statement is in the negative form, the question phrase omits **"not."** Thus we say:

1. { They have a holiday, **haven't they?**
   { They haven't a holiday, **have they?**

2. { You speak English, **don't you?**
   { You don't speak French, **do you?**

3. { He is very tired, **isn't he?**
   { He is not very tired, **is he?**

(See Exercise 37 on page 163.)

168. Misuse of the gerund to express purpose.

Don't say: I come here for learning English.
Say: I come here **to learn** English.

Purpose is commonly expressed by the infinitive, and not by the gerund.

169. "Yes" or "No" in answer to negative questions.

Question: Did you not see the game?
Answer: { **Yes,**—that is, I saw it.
            { **No,**—that is, I did not see it.

In answering negative questions, say **"Yes"** if the answer is an affirmation, and **"No"** if it is a negation; that is, answer without any regard to the negative form of the question.

MISUSED FORMS

170. Using a double negative.

> *Don't say:* He says he is not afraid of nobody.
> *Say:* He says he is **not** afraid of **anybody**.
> *Or:* He says he is afraid of **nobody.**

In English, two negatives are equal to an affirmative statement. You should therefore avoid using two negative words in the same clause: when **"not"** is used, **"none"** changes to **"any,"** **"nothing"** to **"anything,"** **"nobody"** to **"anybody,"** **"no one"** to **"anyone,"** **"nowhere"** to **"anywhere,"** **"neither . . . nor"** to **"either . . . or."**

(See Exercise 39 on page 164.)

171. Using *"one time"* or *"two times"* instead of **"once"** or **"twice."**

> *Don't say:* I was absent one time or two times.
> *Say:* I was absent **once** or **twice**.

"Once" and **"twice"** should be used instead of **"one time"** and **"two times."** But **"thrice"** for **"three times"** is now seldom used.

172. Using *"a day,"* etc., instead of **"one day,"** etc.

> *Don't say:* A day a fox was very hungry.
> *Say:* **One day** a fox was very hungry.

"One" (not **"a"** or **"an"**) should be used with **day, night, morning, afternoon** and **evening,** when the "one" means "a certain."

173. Using *"the other day"* instead of **"the next day,"** etc.

> *Don't say:* He slept well and was better the other day.
> *Say:* He slept well and was better **the next day** (or **on the following day**).

NOTE. **"The other day"** is an idiom meaning a few days ago: as, "I met an old friend **the other day.**"

Have another look at—

NEGATIVES

The negative is generally expressed in two ways:

(1) By putting *not* after the verb. This method is used with only twenty-one verbs. Here is a list of them:

am, is, are, was, were; have, has, had; shall, should; will, would; can, could; may, might; must; need; dare; ought; used.

EXAMPLES: I *am not* ready. You *must not* do that. *He cannot* write well. He *ought not* to go.

(2) By using *do, does, did,* with *not* and the present infinitive (without *to*). This method is used with all verbs except those twenty-one given above. The word order is:

SUBJECT + *do* (*does, did*) + *not* + INFINITIVE

EXAMPLES: I *do not go* there very often. He *does not teach* English. They *did not see* the game.

In conversation, *not* is often shortened to *n't.* Thus we say *don't* for *do not, doesn't* for *does not, didn't* for *did not, hadn't* for *had not, wouldn't* for *would not,* etc. (But we say *shan't* for *shall not, won't* for *will not, can't* for *cannot.*)

Negation may also be expressed by other words of negative meaning: *no, nobody, no one, nothing, nowhere.*

EXAMPLE: They know nothing *or* They do not (don't) know anything.

174. Using *"one and a half,"* etc., instead of **"half past one,"** etc.

Don't say: Lessons begin at seven and a half.
Say: Lessons begin at **half past seven.**

In telling time, we say **"half past one,"** **"half past two,"** **"half past three,"** etc.

175. Using *"as usually"* instead of **"as usual."**

Don't say: As usually, he left his pen at home.
Say: **As usual,** he left his pen at home.

The English phrase **"as usual"** is a shortened form of **"as is usual."** **"As usually"** is not an English phrase at all.

176. Using *"according to my opinion"* instead of **"in my opinion."**

Don't say: According to my opinion, he is right.
Say: **In my opinion,** he is right.

NOTE. Avoid also the use of the phrase **"as I think"** instead of **"I think."** Say: "He is lazy and **I think** he will fail (*not:* as I think)."

177. Using *"at the end"* instead of **"in the end."**

Don't say: At the end they reached the city.
Say: **In the end** they reached the city.

"In the end" means finally or at last; **"at the end"** means at the farthest point or part: as, "There is an index **at the end** of this book." ; "There is a holiday **at the end** of this month."

178. Using *"under the rain"* instead of **"in the rain."**

Don't say: They played football under the rain.
Say: They played football **in the rain.**

NOTE. Also **"in the sun"** and **"in the shade"**: as, "He was sitting **in the sun** (*or* in the shade)."

179. Using *"the reason is because"* instead of **"the reason is that."**

> *Don't say:* The reason is because I believe it.
> *Say:* **The reason is that** I believe it.

The word **"reason"** denotes cause, therefore **"the reason is because"** is a useless repetition. The correct idiom is **"the reason is that . . ."**

180. Using *"a country"* instead of **"the country."**

> *Don't say:* I spend my holidays in a country.
> *Say:* I spend my holidays in **the country.**

"A country" is a place like France, India, or Egypt; **"the country"** is a part of a country consisting of fields, forests, and mountains.

181. Using *"if"* instead of **"whether."**

> *Don't say:* I asked him if he was going.
> *Say:* I asked him **whether** he was going.

Where **"or not"** is implied, **"whether"** must be used, not **"if."** Unlike **"whether,"** **"if"** does not expect a Yes or No reply: as, "I shall speak to him **if** he comes."

182. Using *"any"* for two, instead of **"either."**

> *Don't say:* Any of these two books is good.
> *Say:* **Either** of these two books is good.

"Either" means one or the other of two; **"any"** means one of three or more: as, "**Any** of these books will do."

183. Using *"likes me"* instead of **"I like."**

> *Don't say:* The cinema likes me very much.
> *Say:* **I like** the cinema very much.

NOTE. But "The cinema **appeals to me**" is correct, and means that I like the cinema very much.

MISUSED FORMS

184. Using *"neither . . . or"* instead of **"neither . . . nor."**

Don't say: He speaks neither English or French.

    Say: He speaks **neither** English **nor** French.

REMEMBER that "neither" must be followed by **"nor"** and not by **"or."** But **"either"** is followed by **"or"**: as, "He speaks **either** English **or** French."

185. Using *"both"* in a negative sentence instead of **"neither."**

Don't say: Both of them did not go to school.

    Say: **Neither** of them went to school.

REMEMBER that **"both"** is changed into **"neither"** in a negative sentence.

186. Using *"also"* or *"too"* in a negative sentence instead of **"either."**

Don't say: John has not come also (*or* too).

    Say: John has **not** come **either.**

REMEMBER that **"also"** or **"too"** is changed into **"either"** in a negative sentence.

187. Using *"and"* in a negative sentence instead of **"or."**

Don't say: He did not speak loudly and clearly.

    Say: He did **not** speak loudly **or** clearly.

If a negative word is used in a sentence, the conjunction **"or"** must be used instead of **"and."**

NOTE. But if clauses having different subjects are joined, the conjunction **"and"** is used: as, "He did not write, **and** I did not feel at rest." (Note carefully the use of a comma in front of **"and."**)

188. Using *"till"* instead of **"before"** or **"when."**

Don't say: I had reached the school till the rain started.

    Say: I had reached the school **before** the rain started.

COMMON MISTAKES IN ENGLISH

>   *Or:* I had reached the school **when** the rain
>   started.

A clause of time is introduced by **"before"** or **"when"** instead
of "till," if the verb of the main clause denotes an action
completed before that of the time clause.

UN-ENGLISH EXPRESSIONS

Mistakes often result from too close a translation
into English of foreign idiomatic expressions. The
following are examples of such mistakes:

189. Take an examination, not *give an examination.*

>   *Don't say:* The pupil gave his examination.
>   *Say:* The pupil **took** his examination.

NOTE. The teacher **"gives"** or **"sets"** the examination; the
student **"takes"** the examination or **"sits for"** the examination.

190. To be right or wrong, not *to have right or wrong.*

>   *Don't say:* You have right *or* You have wrong.
>   *Say:* You **are** right *or* You **are** wrong.

191. To be busy, not *to have work.*

>   *Don't say:* I have much work this morning.
>   *Say:* **I am very busy** this morning.

NOTE. But we can say, "**I have a lot of work to do** this morning."

192. It is cold, etc., not *it has cold,* etc.

>   *Don't say:* It has much hot in the summer.
>   *Say:* **It is very hot** in the summer.

193. Take a walk, not *make a walk.*

>   *Don't say:* We made a walk along the river.

Say: We **took** a walk along the river.

NOTE. We can also say: "We **had a walk**" *or* "We **went for a walk** along the river."

194. Go for a ride on a bicycle, etc., not *go for a walk on a bicycle*, etc.

Don't say: We went for a walk on our bicycles.
Say: We went for a **ride** on our bicycles.

NOTE. We "ride" on a bicycle, on horseback, etc., but we "ride" in a bus, train, or other public vehicle.

195. Mount or get on a horse, etc., not *ride a horse*, etc.

Don't say: He rode his bicycle and went home.
Say: He **got on** his bicycle and **rode** home.

NOTE. "To ride" denotes a continuous action; "to mount" or "to get on" denotes a simple action.

196. Dismount or get off a horse, etc., not *come down from a horse*, etc.

Don't say: They came down from their bicycles.
Say: They **got off** their bicycles.

NOTE. We "alight from" or "get out of" a carriage or a motor-car. But we "get on" or "off" the tram, the bus, etc.

197. Go on foot, not *go with the feet*.

Don't say: Shall we go there with the feet?
Say: Shall we go there **on foot**?

198. Take or have a bath, not *make a bath*.

Don't say: I make a shower-bath every morning.
Say: I **take** a shower-bath every morning.
Or: I **have** a shower-bath every morning.

NOTE. But when speaking of the sea or the river, we say: "to bathe," "to have a bathe," "to go for a bathe," "to go bathing"; "to go for a swim" or "to go swimming."

199. Ask a question, not *make a question*.

> *Don't say:* He made me several questions.
> *Say:* He **asked** me several questions.

200. Take an hour, not *need an hour*, etc.

> *Don't say:* I shall need an hour to do that.
> *Say:* **It will take me an hour** to do that.

201. Allow or give a discount, not *make a discount*.

> *Don't say:* He made me a small discount.
> *Say:* He **allowed** me a small discount.
> *Or:* He **gave** me a small discount.

202. Do drill, not *make drill*.

> *Don't say:* We make drill twice a week.
> *Say:* We **do** drill twice a week.

203. Take exercise, not *make exercise*.

> *Don't say:* You ought to make more exercise.
> *Say:* You ought to **take** more exercise.

204. Give or deliver a lecture, not *make a lecture*.

> *Don't say:* He made an interesting lecture.
> *Say:* He **gave** an interesting lecture.
> *Or:* He **delivered** an interesting lecture.

NOTE. But we say, "He **made** an interesting **speech**."

205. Say one's prayers, not *make or do one's prayer*.

> *Don't say:* I make my prayer before I go to bed.
> *Say:* I **say** my prayers before I go to bed.

NOTE. **"To say grace"** is to ask God's blessing before beginning a meal.

206. Pretend, not *make oneself that.*

> *Don't say:* He makes himself that he knows.
> *Say:* He **pretends** to know.

207. Have a dream, not *see a dream.*

> *Don't say:* I saw a strange dream last night.
> *Say:* I **had** a strange dream last night.
> *Or:* I **dreamt** a strange dream last night.

208. Smoke a cigarette, etc., not *drink a cigarette,* etc.

> *Don't say:* He drinks too many cigarettes.
> *Say:* He **smokes** too many cigarettes.

209. Make a mistake, not *do a mistake.*

> *Don't say:* I did one mistake in dictation.
> *Say:* I **made** one mistake in dictation.

210. Tell or speak the truth, not *say the truth.*

> *Don't say:* This man always says the truth.
> *Say:* This man always **tells** the truth.
> *Or:* This man always **speaks** the truth.

NOTE. Also "to tell a lie" (not "to say a lie"): as, "He **told** me a lie."

211. See or watch a game, not *follow a game.*

> *Don't say:* Did you follow the game?
> *Say:* Did you **see** (*or* **watch**) the game?

NOTE. Also avoid saying "to follow the lesson" when you mean "to **attend the class.**"

212. Turn (switch) the light on or off, not *open or shut the light.*

> *Don't say:* Please open (*or* shut) the light.
> *Say:* Please **turn on** (*or* **off**) the light.

Or: Please **switch on** (*or* **off**) the light.

NOTE. But we **"light," "blow out"** or **"put out"** a lamp, a candle, or a fire.

213. Give an example, not *bring an example*.

Don't say: Can you bring a better example?
Say: Can you **give** a better example?

214. Give a mark, not *put a mark*.

Don't say: The teacher put me a good mark.
Say: The teacher **gave** me a good mark.

NOTE. Also avoid: "to put a lesson," "to put a goal," "to put punishment." Say instead: **"to give a lesson," "to score a goal," "to give punishment."**

215. Set a watch by, not *put a watch with*.

Don't say: I put my watch with the church bell.
Say: **I set my watch by** the church bell.

216. A watch is slow or fast, not *goes behind or in front*.

Don't say: My watch goes two minutes behind.
Say: My watch is two minutes **slow.**

NOTE. We can also say, "My watch **loses** or **gains**."

217. Show a film, not *play a film*.

Don't say: This film will be played shortly.
Say: This film will be **shown** shortly.

218. Have one's hair cut, not *cut one's hair*.

Don't say: I am going to cut my hair.
Say: I am going **to have my hair cut.**

NOTE. Also avoid: "I shall make a pair of shoes (or a suit of clothes)." Say instead: **"I shall have a pair of shoes (or a suit of clothes) made."**

219. Learn by heart, not *learn from out*.

> *Don't say:* We have a poem to learn from out.
> *Say:* We have a poem to learn **by heart**.

220. Put on weight, not *put weight*.

> *Don't say:* I have put at least three kilos.
> *Say:* I have **put on** at least three kilos.

NOTE. The opposite of **"put on weight"** is **"to lose weight"**: as, "She has **lost** five kilos."

221. It works miracles, not *it makes miracles*.

> *Don't say:* That medicine makes miracles.
> *Say:* That medicine **works miracles.**

222. Getting on with, not *going with*.

> *Don't say:* How is he going with his work?
> *Say:* How is he **getting on with** his work?

223. This morning, etc., not *today morning*, etc.

> *Don't say:* I have not seen him today morning.
> *Say:* I have not seen him **this morning.**

NOTE. Avoid: "today morning," "today afternoon," "today evening," "yesterday night," "this night." Say: **"this morning," "this afternoon," "this evening," "last night," "tonight."**

224. Quietly, not *slowly, slowly*.

> *Don't say:* The boy came in slowly, slowly.
> *Say:* The boy came in **quietly.**

225. What is the matter? not *What have you?*

> *Don't say:* What have you today?
> *Say:* **What is the matter with you today?**

NOTE. **"What's wrong (with you)?"** and **"What's the trouble (with you)?"** are also correct.

COMMON MISTAKES IN ENGLISH

226. What do you call . . . ? not *How do you call . . . ?*

Don't say: How do you call this in English?
   Say: **What do you call this in English?**

NOTE. But if the question is not about a thing, but about some expression, we should say, **"How do you say this in English?"**

(See Exercise 64 on page 171.)

CHAPTER II

INCORRECT OMISSIONS

OMISSION OF PREPOSITIONS

The following are examples of mistakes made through the omission of the preposition after certain words:

227. Ask for a thing, not *ask a thing*.

Don't say: He came and asked my book.
Say: He came and **asked for** my book.

228. Dispose of a thing, not *dispose a thing*.

Don't say: He will dispose all his property.
Say: He will **dispose of** all his property.

229. Dream of a thing, not *dream a thing*.

Don't say: Young men dream glory and riches.
Say: Young men **dream of** glory and riches.

230. Explain to a person, not *explain a person*.

Don't say: She explained me the matter.
Say: She **explained** the matter **to** me.

231. Knock at the door, not *knock the door*.

Don't say: Who is knocking the door?
Say: Who is **knocking at** the door?

COMMON MISTAKES IN ENGLISH

232. Listen to a person or thing, not *listen a person or thing*.

> *Don't say:* They were listening the music.
> *Say:* They were **listening to** the music.

233. Pay for a thing, not *pay a thing*.

> *Don't say:* How much did you pay the book?
> *Say:* How much did you **pay for** the book?

NOTE. A person can **pay** another person; he can also **pay** a bill, an account, or a subscription; but he **pays for** a thing that he buys.

234. Point to or at a person or thing, not *point a person or thing*.

> *Don't say:* He pointed the map on the wall.
> *Say:* He **pointed to** the map on the wall.
> *Or:* He **pointed at** the map on the wall.

NOTE. Also **"point out"**: as, "He **pointed out** the boy who did it." **"To point"** (without any preposition) means **"to direct"**: as, "Do not **point** the gun this way."

235. Remind a person of something, not *remind a person something*.

> *Don't say:* Please remind me that later.
> *Say:* Please **remind me of** that later.

236. Reply to a person, not *reply a person*.

> *Don't say:* He has not replied me yet.
> *Say:* He has not **replied to** me yet.

237. Say to a person, not *say a person*.

> *Don't say:* He said me, "Come tomorrow."
> *Say:* He **said to** me, "Come tomorrow."

INCORRECT OMISSIONS

238. Search for a lost thing, not *search a lost thing*.

> *Don't say:* They are searching the ball.
> *Say:* They are **searching for** the ball.

NOTE. But **"in search of"**: as, "The wolf goes **in search of** sheep." **"To search"** (without the **"for"**) means to look in one's pockets or house: as, "The policeman **searched** the man and his house."

239. Share with a person, not *share a person*.

> *Don't say:* My friend shared me his book.
> *Say:* My friend **shared** his book **with** me.

240. Speak to a person, not *speak a person*.

> *Don't say:* I shall speak him about that.
> *Say:* I shall **speak to** him about that.

NOTE. "I shall speak **to** him" means "I shall do all the speaking"; "I shall speak **with** him" means "I shall have a conversation with him."

241. Supply a person with something, not *supply a person something*.

> *Don't say:* Can you supply me all I need?
> *Say:* Can you **supply me with** all I need?

NOTE. Also **"provide a person with"**: as, "He **provided his son with** all he needed."

242. Think of a person or thing, not *think a person or thing*.

> *Don't say:* Think a number and then double it.
> *Say:* **Think of** a number and then double it.

243. Wait for a person or thing, not *wait a person or thing*.

> *Don't say:* I shall wait you at the cinema.

Say: I shall **wait for** you at the cinema.

NOTE. But **"await"** takes no preposition: as, "I am **awaiting** your reply."

244. Wish for a thing, not *wish a thing*.

Don't say: He does not wish any reward.
Say: He does not **wish for** any reward.

245. Write to a person, not *write a person*.

Don't say: I shall write him tomorrow.
Say: I shall **write to** him tomorrow.

NOTE. But when the direct object of **"write"** is expressed, the preposition is omitted: as, "I shall **write him a letter**."

(See Exercises 88 and 89 on page 181.)

MISCELLANEOUS EXAMPLES

246. The **"-s"** or **"-es"** of the third person singular omitted.

Don't say: He speak English very well.
Say: **He speaks** English very well.

Great care must be taken not to leave out the **"-s"** or **"-es"** from the present tense, when the subject is **"he," "she," "it,"** or a noun in the singular number.

(See Exercise 32 on page 161.)

247. Using *"don't"* instead of **"doesn't."**

Don't say: He don't care what he says.
Say: **He doesn't** care what he says.

"Don't" (= **"do not"**) is used with **"I," "we," "you," "they,"** and with words that are in the plural number: while **"doesn't"** (= **"does not"**) is used with **"he," "she," "it,"** and with words that are in the singular number.

(See Exercise 33 on page 162.)

Have another look at—

THE THIRD PERSON SINGULAR

1. With the pronouns **he**, **she**, **it**, or any singular noun, the verb in the present tense takes a special ending, *-s* or *-es*: *he works, she sings, it stops, the sun rises.*

2. When the first person of the verb ends in *s*, *x*, *ch*, *sh*, or *o*, the third person singular takes *-es*:

I watch	I finish	I fix	I go
he watches	he finishes	he fixes	he goes

3. When the first person of the verb ends in *-y* with a consonant before it, the third person singular is formed by changing *y* into *ies*:

I carry	I study	I fly
he carries	he studies	he flies

NOTE. If there is a vowel before the *-y*, we add only *s* for the third person singular: *he plays, he enjoys, he obeys.*

4. A few verbs are irregular in the third person singular:

I am	I have	I do	I say
he is	he has	he does	he says

5. The verbs *shall, will, can, may, must,* and *ought* do NOT change their form in the third person singular:

I shall	I will	I can	I may	I must
he shall	he will	he can	he may	he must

REMEMBER: Like the plural of nouns, the third person singular of verbs in the present tense takes *-s* or *-es*.

COMMON MISTAKES IN ENGLISH

248. The **"-d"** or **"-ed"** of the past tense omitted.

> *Don't say:* I receive a letter yesterday.
> *Say:* I **received** a letter yesterday.

Take care not to leave out the **"-d"** or **"-ed"** from the past tense of regular verbs. In speaking, the ending of the past tense should be pronounced clearly.

249. The **"-s"** or **"-es"** of the plural form omitted.

> *Don't say:* I paid six pound for the book.
> *Say:* I paid **six pounds** for the book.

Care must be taken not to leave out the **"-s"** or **"-es"** of the plural number.

NOTE. The following nouns have irregular plurals: **"man, men"**; **"woman, women"**; **"child, children"**; **"ox, oxen"**; **"foot, feet"**; **"tooth, teeth"**; **"goose, geese"**; **"mouse, mice."**

250. The possessive ending omitted.

> *Don't say:* A boy's hat is different from a girl.
> *Say:* A **boy's** hat is different from a **girl's.**

If the first noun in a comparison is in the possessive case, the second must also be in the possessive.

251. Omission of the article before a common noun in the singular.

> *Don't say:* I have no money to buy motor-car.
> *Say:* I have no money to buy **a motor-car.**

As a rule, either **"the"** or **"a"** or **"an"** should be used before a common noun in the singular number.

252. Omission of **"a"** or **"an"** after the verb **"to be."**

> *Don't say:* I am not teacher, I am student.
> *Say:* I am not **a** teacher, I am **a** student.

The indefinite article **"a"** or **"an"** must be used to express a singular noun-complement of the verb **"to be."**

INCORRECT OMISSIONS

253. Omission of **"a"** or **"an"** after the word **"half."**

Don't say: He drank half glass of milk.
Say: He drank **half a glass** of milk.

NOTE. **"Half a glass"** (**"an hour,"** **"a day,"** **"a mile,"** etc.) is the shortened form of **"half of a glass"** (**"of an hour,"** **"of a day,"** **"of a mile,"** etc.).

254. Omission of **"a"** or **"one"** before **"hundred,"** etc.

Don't say: Hundred years make a century.
Say: **A hundred** years make a century.
Or: **One hundred** years make a century.

The indefinite article **"a"** or the numeral **"one"** must be used before **"hundred"** and **"thousand."** See also §543.

255. Omission of **"a"** or **"an"** from **"make a noise,"** etc.

Don't say: I told them not to make noise.
Say: I told them not **to make a noise.**

NOTE. Also **"to make a mistake,"** **"to make a fortune,"** **"to make a will,"** **"to make an impression,"** **"to make an experiment,"** **"to make an attempt."**

(For §§ 251–255 see Exercise 17 on page 155.)

256. Omission of **"the"** before names of nationalities.

Don't say: English are fond of sports.
Say: **The English** are fond of sports.

The definite article must be placed before the names of nationalities, describing a people collectively: as, "the British," "**the** French," "**the** Dutch," "**the** Swiss," "**the** Chinese," "**the** Sudanese," etc.

55

Have another look at—
THE INDEFINITE ARTICLE

The indefinite article is used:

(1) Before every common noun in the singular, if it is not preceded by *the* or some word such as *this, that, my, his*: as, "I bought *a* new book" (*not:* I bought new book).

(2) Before the words *hundred* and *thousand*: as, "*A* hundred soldiers were in the camp."

(3) After the verb *to be* when a common noun in the singular follows: as, "Mary's father is *a* lawyer."

(4) In certain phrases: as, to make *a* noise, *a* mistake, *a* fortune, *an* impression; to have *a* headache, *a* pain, *a* cold, *a* cough.

The indefinite article is not used:

(1) Before singular nouns that are not used in the plural, such as *advice, information, work, furniture, bread*: as, "He gave me good advice" (*not*: a good advice).

(2) After the phrase **"kind of"** or **"sort of"**: as, "What kind of pen do you want?"

A, AN or ONE

In many languages the numeral **"one"** is used instead of the indefinite article **"a"** or **"an."** This is not so in English. "One man went into one shop" ought to be "**A** man went into **a** shop." **"One"** is to be used only when the *number* is emphatic: as, **"One** swallow does not make a summer."

INCORRECT OMISSIONS

257. Omission of **"the"** before names of musical instruments.

> *Don't say:* I play violin, but not piano.
> *Say:* I play **the violin,** but not **the piano.**

The definite article should be used before the names of musical instruments.

258. Omission of **"the"** before the word **"cinema,"** etc.

> *Don't say:* On Saturday I go to cinema.
> *Say:* On Saturday **I go to the cinema.**

The definite article is required before the words **"cinema," "theatre," "concert,"** etc.

259. Omission of **"the"** before the names of ships.

> *Don't say:* Nelson is a British warship.
> *Say:* **The Nelson** is a British warship.

The definite article should be inserted before the names of ships: as, **"the Queen Elizabeth," "the Mohammed Ali," "the Crete."**

NOTE. In English, ships are spoken of as if feminine and are referred to with the pronouns **"she"** and **"her"**: as, "The **Hood** went down with all **her** crew."

260. Omission of the verb **"to be"** from the passive.

> *Don't say:* Charles Dickens born in 1812.
> *Say:* Charles Dickens **was born** in 1812.

The passive voice is always formed by the use of the verb **"to be,"** combined with the past participle of the verb required (**"to be"** + past participle).

261. Omission of the auxiliary **"do"** from questions.

> *Don't say:* { You understand the problem?
> He understands the problem?
> He understood the problem?

Have another look at—

THE VERB "TO BE"

Present Tense	I **am**, you **are**, he (she, it) **is**; We, you, they **are**.
Past Tense	I **was**, you **were**, he (she, it) **was**; We, you, they **were**.
Future Tense	I **shall be**, you, he (she, it) **will be**; We **shall be**, you, they **will be**.
Present Perfect	I, you **have been**, he (she, it) **has been**; We, you, they **have been**.
Past Perfect	I, you, he (she, it) **had been**; We, you, they **had been**.
Future Perfect	I **shall have been**, you, he (she, it) **will have been**; We **shall have been**, you, they **will have been**.

*   *   *

USES OF THE VERB *TO BE*

The verb *to be* is used:

(1) With the Present Participle to form the Continuous Tenses.

To be + Present Participle

EXAMPLE: The sun *was shining* in the sky.

(2) With the Past Participle to form the Passive Voice.

To be + Past Participle

EXAMPLE: The letter *was written* by John.

INCORRECT OMISSIONS

Say:
> **Do you understand** the problem?
> **Does he understand** the problem?
> **Did he understand** the problem?

The auxiliary verb **"do"** (**"does," "did"**) is placed before another verb to ask questions in the present and past tenses.

NOTE. But the auxiliary **"do"** should not be used with verbs which are themselves auxiliaries, like **"can," "may," "must"**: as, "**Can** you meet me tomorrow?"

(See Exercise 36 on page 163.)

262. Omission of **"do"** when it is a principal verb.

Don't say: Do pupils their work carefully?
Say: **Do** pupils **do** their work carefully?

In the correct form of the sentence, the first **"do"** has no meaning of its own and only helps to make the question; whereas the second **"do"** is the principal verb of the sentence, and has the meaning of **"perform."**

263. Omission of the preposition indicating time.

Don't say: I was born the third of December.
Say: I was born **on the third** of December.

As a rule, a noun should not be used without a preposition to show the time of some action.

NOTE. But no preposition is used with **"last year," "next year," "some day," "one day," "any day," "that day," "this afternoon,"** etc.

264. Omission of the preposition after the infinitive.

Don't say: They have no houses to live.
Say: They have no houses **to live in.**

If the infinitive is of an intransitive verb (like **"live,"** etc.), it must have a preposition after it. The object of the preposition is omitted.

265. Omission of **"there"** as an introductory word.

Don't say: Once lived a great king.

Say: Once **there lived** a great king.

The adverb "**there**" should be used to introduce the subject of a sentence in which the verb stands before the subject.

266. Omission of "how" after the verb "to know."

Don't say: She knows to play the piano.
Say: She **knows how to play** the piano.

After the verb "**to know**" the infinitive is always introduced by the adverb "**how**."

267. Omission of "should" after the word "lest."

Don't say: He ran lest he miss the train.
Say: He ran **lest he should** miss the train.

"**Lest**" (= in order that . . . not) is generally followed by the word "**should**."

268. Omission of "other" after a comparative.

Don't say: Homer was greater than all the Greek poets.
Say: Homer was greater than all the **other** Greek poets.

Since Homer was a Greek poet, the first sentence makes him greater than himself, which is illogical.

269. Omission of "before" in comparisons.

Don't say: I had never seen such a thing.
Say: I had never seen such a thing **before.**

The word "**before**" should not be left out in making a comparison between one thing and all others of the same kind.

270. Omission of "else" after "everybody", etc.

Don't say: He is stronger than anybody.
Say: He is stronger than **anybody else.**

In making a comparison between one person or thing and all others of the same kind, the word "**else**" must be used after "**everybody**," "**anybody**," "**anything**," etc.

INCORRECT OMISSIONS

271. The demonstrative pronoun **"one"** omitted.

> *Don't say:* This is the only that I like.
> *Say:* This is the only **one** that I like.

The demonstrative pronoun **"one"** (plural **"ones"**) is used in place of a noun mentioned before.

272. Omission of the personal pronoun before the infinitive.

> *Don't say:* I want to tell me the truth.
> *Say:* **I want you to tell** me the truth.

With verbs like **"want," "like," "wish,"** etc., the subject of the infinitive is expressed if it is different from that of the main verb.

273. Omission of **"it"** as subject of an impersonal verb.

> *Don't say:* Is very hot in the Sudan.
> *Say:* **It** is very hot in the Sudan.

The pronoun **"it"** as the subject of an impersonal verb should be expressed.

274. Omission of the pronoun subject from the principal clause.

> *Don't say:* When he saw the teacher, stood up.
> *Say:* When he saw the teacher, **he** stood up.

In a sentence beginning with an adverbial clause, the personal pronoun as the subject of the principal clause must be expressed.

275. Omission of the personal pronoun after a quotation.

> *Don't say:* "I am learning English," said.
> *Say:* "I am learning English," **he** said.

After a quotation, the personal pronoun as the subject of the reporting verb must be expressed.

276. The object of the transitive verb omitted.

> *Don't say:* I asked him for some paper, but he had not.
>
> > *Say:* I asked him for some paper, but he had **none.**

As a rule, every transitive verb must have an expressed object: here, **"none"** (equivalent to "not any") is the object of **"had."**

277. Omission of the direct object when there are two objects.

> *Don't say:* I asked him for some ink, and he gave me.
>
> > *Say:* I asked him for some ink, and he gave me **some.**

Some transitive verbs, like **"give," "bring," "send," "tell," "buy," "show,"** must have two expressed objects, direct and indirect: here, **"some"** is the direct object of **"gave."**

278. The object of the verb **"enjoy"** omitted.

> *Don't say:* I enjoyed during the holidays.
> *Say:* **I enjoyed myself** during the holidays.
> *Or:* **I enjoyed my holidays.**

The verb **"enjoy"** cannot be followed by a preposition. It must always have an object, which may be either a reflexive pronoun or a noun.

NOTE. We also say: **"I had a good time"** (= I enjoyed myself); but not "I enjoyed my time."

279. Omission of the noun after an adjective.

> *Don't say:* The unfortunate was shot dead.
> *Say:* The **unfortunate man** was shot dead.

The noun coming after an adjective cannot be understood; it must be expressed.

NOTE. The noun is omitted after an adjective only when the adjective is used **as a noun in the plural**: as, **"The poor** envy **the rich."**

INCORRECT OMISSIONS

280. Omission of the word **"and"** between numbers.

Don't say: Eight thousand thirty-seven.
    Say: Eight thousand **and** thirty-seven.

The conjunction **"and"** must be used to connect **"hundred," "thousand," "million"** to a number of tens or units.

281. Omission of the word **"or"** between numbers.

Don't say: I have only two, three friends.
    Say: I have only **two or three** friends.

We must always insert the conjunction **"or"** between numbers used thus: **"two or three men," "five or six pages," "eight or ten days."**

282. Omission of the word **"old"** from age.

Don't say: My sister is fifteen years.
    Say: My sister is **fifteen years old.**

NOTE. We may also say, "My sister is **fifteen years of age,**" or simply, "My sister is **fifteen.**"

283. *"For this"* used instead of **"for this reason."**

Don't say: For this he wants to leave.
    Say: **For this reason** he wants to leave.

The phrase **"for this"** is incorrect. Say **"for this reason"** or **"for that reason"**; also **"owing to that"** or **"because of that."**

284. *"To these"* used instead of **"to these words."**

Don't say: To these, he replied ——
    Say: **To these words,** he replied ——

The phrase **"to these"** is incorrect. Say, **"to these words"** or **"to this."**

285. *"Better"* used instead of **"had better."**

Don't say: Better go home at once.
    Say: **You had better go** home at once.

The correct phrase is **"had better." "You had better go"** means **"It would be a good thing for you to go."**

COMMON MISTAKES IN ENGLISH

286. "*Up*" and "*down*" used instead of **"upstairs"** and **"downstairs."**

> *Don't say:* He is up; he is down.
> *Say:* He is **upstairs**; he is **downstairs**.

"He is up" means he is out of bed. **"He is upstairs (downstairs)"** means he is on the upper (lower) floor of the building.

287. "*Throw it*" used instead of **"throw it away."**

> *Don't say:* It is dirty; throw it.
> *Say:* It is dirty; **throw it away**.

"Throw it" means to throw a thing to someone, such as a ball. **"Throw it away"** means to get rid of it by throwing it aside.

288. "*I don't think*" used instead of **"I don't think so."**

> *Don't say.* I don't think.
> *Say:* **I don't think so.**

"I don't think" means I do not use my brains; while **"I don't think so"** means I am not of that opinion.

289. "*Before yesterday*," etc., used instead of **"the day before yesterday,"** etc.

> *Don't say:* He arrived before yesterday.
> *Say:* He arrived **the day before yesterday**.

The phrases "before yesterday," "after tomorrow," "after next week" are incorrect. Say instead, **"the day before yesterday," "the day after tomorrow," "the week after next."**

290. "*Thank you*" used instead of **"No, thank you."**

> *Don't say:* Thank you (if you want to refuse an offer).
> *Say:* **No, thank you.**

NOTE. **"Thank you"** is used to accept an offer, and generally means **"Yes, please."**

Chapter III

UNNECESSARY WORDS

UNNECESSARY PREPOSITIONS

The words below do not require a preposition to go with them because they have within them the meaning of the preposition.

291. Answer (= **reply to**).

> *Don't say:* Please answer to my question.
> *Say:* Please **answer my question.**

NOTE. But the noun **"answer"** takes **"to"**: as, "His **answer to** my question was wrong."

292. Approach (= **come near to**).

> *Don't say:* Do not approach to that house.
> *Say:* Do not **approach that house.**

293. Ask (= **put a question to**).

> *Don't say:* I asked to the teacher about it.
> *Say:* I **asked the teacher** about it.

294. Attack (= **go and fight against**).

> *Don't say:* They attacked against the enemy.
> *Say:* They **attacked the enemy.**

NOTE. But we say, **"to make an attack on"**: as, "They **made an attack on** the enemy."

295. Comprise (= consist of).

Don't say: The book comprises of five chapters.
Say: The book **comprises five chapters.**

296. Enter (= go into).

Don't say: We entered into the classroom.
Say: We **entered the classroom.**

NOTE. But we enter **"into"** a conversation, a debate, or a discussion.

297. Finish (= come to the end of).

Don't say: I have finished from my work.
Say: I have **finished my work.**

298. Leave (= depart from).

Don't say: He left from England last week.
Say: He **left England** last week.

299. Obey (= act according to).

Don't say: We should obey to our teachers.
Say: We should **obey our teachers.**

300. Permit (= give permission to).

Don't say: He permitted to him to stay here.
Say: He **permitted him** to stay here.

NOTE. **"Allow"** is similar in meaning and use to **"permit"**: as, "He **allowed him** to stay here."

301. Reach (= arrive at).

Don't say: We reached at the school early.
Say: We **reached the school** early.

302. Resemble (= be similar to).

Don't say: Does he resemble to his father?

UNNECESSARY WORDS

Say: Does he **resemble his father?**

NOTE. But **"resemblance"** takes **"to"** or **"between"**: as, "He has no **resemblance to** his father"; "There is no **resemblance between** them."

303. Tell (= say to).

Don't say: I told to him to come at once.
Say: I **told him** to come at once

304. Behind (= at the back of).

Don't say: He hid behind of a large tree.
Say: He hid **behind a large tree.**

305. Inside (= on the inner side of).

Don't say: The boys went inside of the room.
Say: The boys went **inside the room.**

306. Outside (= out of).

Don't say: They stood outside of the door.
Say: They stood **outside the door.**

307. Round (= on all sides of).

Don't say: The earth goes round of the sun.
Say: The earth goes **round the sun.**

NOTE. **"Around"** is similar in meaning and use to **"round."**

(See Exercises 90 and 91 on pages 181–182.)

UNNECESSARY ARTICLES

308. Wrong use of "*the*" with proper nouns.

Don't say: The George will go to the England.
Say: **George** will go to **England.**

As a rule, the definite article is not used with proper nouns.

NOTE. But **"the"** is generally placed before the names of (1) rivers, (2) seas, (3) oceans, (4) bays, (5) gulfs, (6) mountain ranges, (7) groups of islands, and (8) countries or provinces consisting of an adjective and a noun. Thus we say: "**the** Nile," "**the** Mediterranean," "**the** Atlantic," "**the** Bay of Biscay," "**the** Persian Gulf," "**the** Alps," "**the** Dodecanese," "**the** United States," "**the** Central Provinces (of India)."

309. Wrong use of "*the*" with proper nouns in the possessive.

Don't say: The Euripides' tragedies are famous.
Say: **Euripides'** tragedies are famous.

The definite article must not be used with proper nouns in the possessive case.

NOTE. With foreign names the extra syllable marking the possessive is often awkward to pronounce: the apostrophe only is then used, as in **"Euripides' tragedies."**

310. Wrong use of "*the*" with abstract nouns.

Don't say: The bravery is a great virtue.
Say: **Bravery** is a great virtue.

Abstract nouns, **if used in a general sense,** cannot take the article.

NOTE. But if abstract nouns are used in a particular sense they require the use of the article: as, "**The bravery of the Spartans** was renowned."

311. Wrong use of "*the*" with material nouns.

Don't say: The gold is a precious metal.
Say: **Gold** is a precious metal.

Material nouns, **if used in a general sense,** are used without any article.

NOTE. If, however, material nouns are used in a particular sense, the definite article is required: as, "**The gold of South Africa** is exported to many countries."

312. Wrong use of "*the*" with plural nouns used in a general sense.

Don't say: The dogs are faithful animals.

UNNECESSARY WORDS

Say: **Dogs** are faithful animals.

The definite article is omitted before common nouns in the plural **if used in a general sense.**

313. Wrong use of "*the*" with names of languages.

Don't say: He speaks the English very well.
Say: **He speaks English** very well.

The definite article is never used before the names of languages.

NOTE. But we can say, "He speaks **the English language** very well."

314. Wrong use of "*the*" with names of meals.

Don't say: We shall start after the breakfast.
Say: We shall start **after breakfast.**

The definite article should **not** be used before the names of the meals—**"breakfast," "lunch," "dinner,"** or **"supper."**

315. Wrong use of "*the*" with names of games.

Don't say: My favourite game is the football.
Say: My favourite game is **football.**

No article is used before the names of games like **"football," "hockey," "tennis," "cricket," "volley-ball," "basket-ball."**

316. Wrong use of "*the*" with names of diseases.

Don't say: The cholera is a dreadful disease.
Say: **Cholera** is a dreadful disease.

As a rule, the definite article is **not** used before the names of diseases.

NOTE. But the article is needed with common names of illnesses: as, "I was suffering from **a cold (a fever, a cough, a headache).**"

317. Wrong use of "*the*" with names of colours.

Don't say: The green is a beautiful colour.

Say: **Green** is a beautiful colour.

The definite article should **not** be used before the names of colours **when used as nouns.**

318. Wrong use of "*the*" with the names of the senses.

Don't say: The smell is one of the five senses.
Say: **Smell** is one of the five senses.

No article is used before the names of the five senses: **"sight,"** **"smell," "hearing," "taste,"** and **"touch."**

319. Wrong use of "*the*" with names of days and months.

Don't say: {The Sunday is a day of prayer.
{The December is the last month.

Say: {**Sunday** is a day of prayer.
{**December** is the last month.

The definite article should **not** be used before the names of days and months.

NOTE. But we say **"the Sunday before last," "the December of 1940,"** etc.

320. Wrong use of "*the*" with **"man"** denoting the human race.

Don't say: The man is born a sinner.
Say: **Man** is born a sinner.

"Man", denoting the human race, is used without the definite article. So also **"mankind"** requires no article: as, "Disease is the enemy of **mankind.**"

321. Wrong use of "*the*" with **"school."**

Don't say: My brother goes to the school.
Say: My brother **goes to school.**

"To go to school" means **to be a student**; while **"to go to the school"** means **to visit the school.**

NOTE. Similarly, **"to leave school"** means **to stop being a student**; and **"to leave the school"** means **to go away from** the school premises.

70

322. Wrong use of "*the*" with "**church.**"

Don't say: On Sunday I go to the church.
Say: On Sunday **I go to church.**

"**To go to church**" means **to go and pray**; while "**to go to the church**" means **to go and visit the church.**

NOTE. Similarly, distinguish between "**go to bed**" and "**go to the bed,**" "**go to prison**" and "**go to the prison,**" "**go to market**" and "**go to the market,**" "**go to sea**" and "**go to the sea,**" "**go to hospital**" and "**go to the hospital,**" "**sit at table**" and "**sit at the table.**"

323. Wrong use of "*the*" with "**nature.**"

Don't say: The nature is beautiful in spring.
Say: **Nature** is beautiful in spring.

NOTE. But the definite article is required if "**nature**" is used in other meanings: as, "It is in **the nature** of a dog to be faithful."

324. Wrong use of "*the*" with "**society.**"

Don't say: A thief is a danger to the society.
Say: A thief is a danger to **society.**

NOTE. But the definite article is required if "**society**" is used (1) in a particular sense: as, "**The society** of the Greeks was based on freedom"; (2) in the sense of companionship: as, "I enjoy **the society** of my friends."

325. Wrong use of "*the*" in the phrase "**in future**" (= from now on).

Don't say: You must be careful in the future.
Say: You must be careful **in future.**

NOTE. "**In the future**" means in the time to come: as, "Nobody knows what will happen **in the future.**"

326. Wrong use of "*the*" after "**whose.**"

Don't say: The boy whose the father is ill has left.

71

Say: The boy **whose father** is ill has left.

The article must not be used after the relative **"whose"** because the relative takes the place of the article.

327. Wrong use of the indefinite article after **"kind of"** or **"sort of."**

Don't say: What kind of a book do you want?
Say: What **kind of book** do you want?

The phrase **"kind of"** or **"sort of"** should not be followed by the indefinite article **"a"** or **"an."**

328. Wrong use of the indefinite article before **"work,"** etc.

Don't say: He now found a work at the bank.
Say: He now **found work** at the bank.

The indefinite article should not be used before such words as **"work," "fun," "health," "permission."**

(See Exercise 18 on page 155.)

THE INFINITIVE WITHOUT "TO"

Mistakes are frequently made by using the infinitive sign **"to"** after the following verbs, which do not require it.

329. Can + infinitive without "to."

Don't say: My brother can to swim very well.
Say: My brother **can swim** very well.

NOTE. The negative form **"cannot"** is always written as one word.

330. Could + infinitive without "to."

Don't say: I could not to see you yesterday.
Say: I **could** not **see** you yesterday.

Have another look at—

THE DEFINITE ARTICLE

As a rule, nouns in English take no article when used *in a general sense*, but if they are used *in a particular sense* the article is needed. Note the difference in the use or omission of the article:

(1) With plural nouns:

> *Horses* are strong animals.
> *The horses* in the field belong to the farmer.

(2) With abstract nouns:

> *Wisdom* is a great virtue.
> *The wisdom* of Solomon was famous.

(3) With material nouns:

> *Water* is necessary to life.
> *The water* in the kitchen is hot.

(4) With days, months, and seasons:

> *Summer* is a hot season.
> *The summer* of last year was very hot.

(5) With names of languages:

> *English* is spoken all over the world.
> *The English* spoken by him is not correct.

(6) With names of meals:

> *Breakfast* is at eight o'clock.
> *The breakfast* I had this morning was heavy.

(7) With names of colours:

> *Blue* is my favourite colour.
> *The blue* in that picture has faded.

331. May + infinitive without "to."

Don't say: May I to trouble you for a moment?
Say: **May I trouble** you for a moment?

332. Might + infinitive without "to."

Don't say: He might to come in the morning.
Say: He **might come** in the morning.

333. Must + infinitive without "to."

Don't say: I must to see him at his office.
Say: I **must see** him at his office.

334. Let + infinitive without "to."

Don't say: His father would not let him to go.
Say: His father would not **let him go.**

335. Make (to force) + infinitive without "to."

Don't say: You can't make him to understand.
Say: You can't **make him understand.**

336. See + infinitive without "to."

Don't say: They saw him to leave the house.
Say: They **saw him leave** the house.

NOTE. "They saw him **leaving** the house" is also correct.

337. Watch + infinitive without "to."

Don't say: I watched the boys to play hockey.
Say: I **watched the boys play** hockey.

NOTE. "I watched the boys **playing** hockey" is also correct.

338. Hear + infinitive without "to."

Don't say: We heard him to speak in English.
Say: We **heard him speak** in English.

NOTE. "We heard him **speaking** in English" is also correct.

UNNECESSARY WORDS

339. Feel + infinitive without "to."

Don't say: I could feel his heart to beat.
Say: I could **feel his heart beat.**
Or: I could **feel his heart beating.**

NOTE. If the verbs **"make," "see," "watch," "hear," "feel,"** are used in the passive, the sign **"to"** must be used: as, "He was seen **to leave** the house"; "He was heard **to speak** in English."

(See Exercise 67 on page 173.)

MISCELLANEOUS EXAMPLES

340. Wrong repetition of subject.

Don't say: My little brother he is at school.
Say: **My little brother** is at school.

Never repeat the subject by using a pronoun after the noun. **"My little brother"** and **"he"** denote the same person: therefore, one or the other may be used as subject, but not both.

341. Wrong repetition of subject in a compound sentence.

Don't say: I went to market and I bought fruit.
Say: **I** went to market and bought fruit.

In a compound sentence, the same subject is expressed once only and is not repeated before each verb, unless the sentence is long and complicated.

342. Wrong repetition of subject after an adjectival clause.

Don't say: George, who is a careless pupil, he lost his book.
Say: **George,** who is a careless pupil, **lost his book.**

If the subordinate clause is an enlargement of the subject, the personal pronoun should not be used before the verb of the principal clause.

75

343. Wrong repetition of subject after a participial phrase.

> *Don't say:* The man having finished his work he received his pay.
>
> *Say:* **The man** having finished his work **received his pay.**

When a participial phrase is used after a noun subject, the finite verb must not be preceded by a personal pronoun.

344. Wrong use of personal pronoun in a relative clause.

> *Don't say:* The book which I lost it was new.
>
> *Say:* The book **which I lost** was new.

A personal pronoun as well as a relative cannot be used in the relative clause **if they both refer to the same antecedent.** In the first sentence both **"which"** and **"it"** refer to **"book."**

345. Wrong repetition of object.

> *Don't say:* The doctor I know him very well.
>
> *Say:* **I know the doctor** very well.

In the sentence given, the words **"doctor"** and **"him"** denote one and the same object: therefore, either **"doctor"** or **"him"** may be used, but not both in the same sentence.

346. Wrong repetition of object with infinitive.

> *Don't say:* I bought an English book to read it.
>
> *Say:* I bought an English book **to read.**

An object cannot be repeated with an infinitive of purpose **if the verb takes an object.**

(For §§ 340–346 see Exercise 21 on page 157.)

347. Wrong use of "*that*" in direct speech.

> *Don't say:* He said that, "I am sure to pass."
>
> *Say:* **He said,** "I am sure to pass."

We cannot use **"that"** in direct speech: that is, when we repeat without any change the words that some other person has spoken.

NOTE. But in indirect speech we say: **"He said that he was sure to pass."**

348. Using a double comparative.

Don't say: He is more stronger than George.
　　Say: He is **stronger** than George.

Double comparatives are incorrect: "more stronger" ought to be only **"stronger."** However, we can say **"much stronger."**

349. Misuse of adjectives that cannot be compared.

Don't say: My work is more perfect than his.
　　Say: My work is **superior** to his.
　　Or: My work is **better** than his.

Certain adjectives cannot be compared: **perfect, unique, preferable, supreme, right,** etc.

350. *"Return back"* used instead of **"return."**

Don't say: She has returned back to school.
　　Say: She has **returned** to school.

The word **"back"** cannot be used with **"return,"** since **"return"** means **to come back.**

351. *"Have got"* used instead of **"have."**

Don't say: He has got blue eyes and red hair.
　　Say: He **has** blue eyes and red hair.

"Get" means **to acquire; "has got"** should therefore not be used unless the intended meaning is **has acquired**: as, "He **has got** his reward at last."

NOTE. In conversation, however, it is more idiomatic to say, "He **has got** blue eyes and red hair."

352. *"Begin from"* used instead of **"begin."**

Don't say: Examinations begin from Thursday.
　　Say: Examinations **begin on Thursday.**

A thing can **begin** only at a point of time. The word cannot be used to apply to the whole time during which a thing is being done.

353. *"Consider as"* used instead of **"consider."**

> *Don't say:* He considers me as his best friend.
> *Say:* He **considers me his best friend**.

The word **"consider"** cannot be followed by **"as."** But we say, "He **regards me as his best friend**."

354. *"For to"* used instead of **"to."**

> *Don't say:* I came here for to learn English.
> *Say:* I came here **to learn** English.

The preposition **"for"** should never be put before the sign **"to"** of the infinitive.

355. *"From where"* used instead of **"where."**

> *Don't say:* From where can I buy a good watch?
> *Say:* **Where** can I buy a good watch?

"Where" means **at what place**; while **"from where"** denotes the point of origin: as, **"From where** do tourists come?"

356. *"And etc."* used instead of **"etc."**

> *Don't say:* I, you, we, and etc. are pronouns.
> *Say:* I, you, we, **etc.,** are pronouns.

"Etc." is the short form of **"et cetera,"** a Latin phrase meaning **and other things**. The combination **"and etc."** is wrong because it would mean **and and other things**.

NOTE. However, students are advised to avoid using **"etc."** in a composition and to use instead of it phrases such as **"and other things," "and the rest," "and so on."**

357. *"So . . . so that"* used instead of **"so . . . that."**

> *Don't say:* I am so tired so that I cannot go.
> *Say:* I am **so tired that** I cannot go.

When **"so"** or **"such"** is completed by a clause of result, the clause is introduced by **"that"** and not by **"so that."**

UNNECESSARY WORDS

358. *"From now and on"* used instead of **"from now on."**

> *Don't say:* From now and on I will study hard.
> *Say:* **From now on** I will study hard.

The phrase "from now and on" is incorrect. Say, **"from now on."**

359. *"Though . . . yet"* used instead of **"though."**

> *Don't say:* Though it is raining, yet he will go.
> *Say:* Though it is raining, **he will go.**

"Though" (**"although"**) is the conjunction introducing the subordinate clause, and a second one (**"yet"** or **"still"**) is not required.

360. *"Go to home"* used instead of **"go home."**

> *Don't say:* When school is over I go to home.
> *Say:* When school is over **I go home.**

The expression "I go to home" is wrong. Say, **"I go home."**

361. Using *"far"* with a phrase of definite distance.

> *Don't say:* He lives two miles far from here.
> *Say:* He lives **two miles from here.**

When a phrase of definite distance (like **"two miles"**) is used in a sentence, the word **"far"** cannot be used also. But we can say, "He lives **two miles away.**"

CHAPTER IV

MISPLACED WORDS

WRONG POSITION OF ADVERBS

362. The adverb of definite time misplaced.

> *Don't say:* I last night went to the cinema
> *Say:* I went to the cinema **last night.**

Adverbs or adverbial phrases of definite time, like **"yesterday," "today," "tomorrow," "last week," "two months ago,"** are usually placed at the end of the sentence. But if we wish to emphasize the time, we place the adverb at the beginning: as, **"Yesterday** I was very busy."

NOTE. If there is more than one adverb of definite time in a sentence, we put the more exact expression before the more general: as, "He was born **at two o'clock in the morning on April 12th in the year 1942.**"

363. The adverb of indefinite time misplaced.

> *Don't say:* They come always late to school.
> *Say:* They **always come** late to school.

Adverbs of indefinite time, like **"ever," "never," "always," "often," "seldom," "soon," "sometimes,"** and the adverbs **"almost," "scarcely," "hardly," "nearly," "even,"** are placed before the principal verb.

NOTE. But with the verb **"to be"** the adverb of indefinite time is placed **after** the verb: as, "They **are always** late."

364. The adverb of time placed before the adverb of place.

> *Don't say:* Our boys will be tomorrow here.

MISPLACED WORDS

Say: Our boys will be **here tomorrow.**

If an adverb of time and an adverb of place are used together in a sentence, the adverb of place must come first.

365. The adverb misplaced with a transitive verb.

Don't say: He wrote carefully his exercise.
Say: He wrote his exercise **carefully.**

With a transitive verb, the adverb generally comes after the object.

NOTE. If, however, the object is long, the adverb may come after the transitive verb: as, "He wrote **carefully** all the exercises he had to do."

366. The adverb **"only"** misplaced.

Don't say: I only saw him once after that.
Say: I saw him **only once** after that.

"Only" should be placed immediately before the word which it qualifies. (Here **"only"** qualifies the adverb **"once,"** and not the verb **"saw."**)

(See Exercise 69 on page 173.)

367. The adverb **"enough"** misplaced.

Don't say: Is the room enough large for you?
Say: Is the room **large enough** for you?

The adverb **"enough"** is placed after the word which it qualifies and not before it.

NOTE. But the adjective **"enough"** may come either before or after the noun: as, "We have **enough food** for six people"; *or* "We have **food enough** for six people."

368. **"Not"** misplaced with a compound verb.

Don't say: I should have not gone . . .
Say: I should **not** have gone . . .

The position of **"not"** in a compound verb is after the first auxiliary.

COMMON MISTAKES IN ENGLISH

NOTE. But with the present or perfect participle, **"not"** is placed at the beginning: as, "**Not** having done his work, he was punished"; "**Not** being rich, he could not afford it."

369. "Not" misplaced with the negative infinitive.

Don't say: I told him to not come on Monday.
Say: I told him **not to come** on Monday.

The position of **"not"** in the negative infinitive is immediately before the word **"to,"** and not after it.

(See Exercises 68 and 70 on pages 173–174.)

370. The subject of the sentence misplaced.

Don't say: Last week visited our school a man.
Say: **A man** visited our school last week.

In most English sentences the subject is placed **first**, the verb next, then the object, with the rest following.

371. The subject misplaced in questions.

Don't say: {You were at the cinema yesterday?
{They will come with us tomorrow?
Say: {**Were you** at the cinema yesterday?
{**Will they** come with us tomorrow?

In interrogative sentences, the subject is generally placed after the verb. If the tense is compound, the subject comes after the auxiliary, and the rest follows.

NOTE. Exception to this rule is occasionally made in spoken English, but students are advised to follow the rule.

372. The subject misplaced in questions beginning with an interrogative word.

Don't say: Why you were absent last Friday?
Say: Why **were you** absent last Friday?

In questions beginning with an interrogative word, like **what,** when, where, why, how, the verb is placed before the subject as in all questions.

(For §§ 371–372 see Exercise 36 on page 163.)

373. The subject misplaced after **"never,"** etc.

Don't say: Never I have heard of such a thing.
Say: Never **have I heard** of such a thing.

When **"never," "seldom," "rarely," "neither," "nor," "not only," "no sooner,"** are placed at the beginning of a complete clause, the verb must come before the subject as in a question.

374. *"All . . . not"* used instead of **"Not all."**

Don't say: All people are not hard-working.
Say: **Not all** people are hard-working.

The first sentence is wrong because it makes *all* people lazy.

NOTE. Similarly, "Everybody does not like dancing" should be "**Not everybody** likes dancing."

375. The subject misplaced in indirect questions.

Don't say: He asked me what games did I play?
Say: He asked me what games **I played.**

In indirect questions the usual order of words is followed: subject first and then verb.

(See Exercise 38 on page 164.)

376. The direct object misplaced.

Don't say: He touched with his hand the ball.
Say: He **touched the ball** with his hand.

The object of a transitive verb generally comes **directly after the verb.**

377. The indirect object misplaced.

Don't say: I showed to him some of my stamps.
Say: I showed some of my stamps **to him.**

Have another look at—

QUESTIONS

Questions can be formed in three ways:

(1) By putting the verb before the subject. This method is used only with twenty-one verbs. Here is a list of them:

am, is, are, was, were; have, has, had; shall, should; will, would; can, could; may, might; must; need; dare; ought; used.

EXAMPLES: Are you ready? Can you write well? Will he come tomorrow? May I go now?

(2) By using *do, does, did,* followed by the subject and then the infinitive (without *to*). This form is used with all verbs except the twenty-one given above. The word order is:

Do (*does, did*) + SUBJECT + INFINITIVE

EXAMPLES: Do you come here every day? Does the boy learn English? Did they go to the theatre?

(3) By using question words. The question word always begins the question, but the verb must be put before the subject as in questions of types (1) and (2).

EXAMPLES: Why are you late? When did you come? Where is it? Whom did you see? Which book do you want?

If the question word is the subject of the sentence, the verb is put *after* the subject: as, Who wrote the letter? Whose dog bit the man?

MISPLACED WORDS

If the indirect object is preceded by a preposition, it is placed after the direct object.

NOTE. But the indirect object usually comes first **without a preposition**: as, "I showed **him** some of my stamps."

378. The qualifying adjective misplaced.

> *Don't say:* My uncle has a garden very large.
> *Say:* My uncle has a very **large garden.**

The adjective is generally put immediately before the noun it qualifies.

379. The past participle misplaced.

> *Don't say:* The ordered goods have not arrived.
> *Say:* The **goods ordered** have not arrived.

"The goods ordered" is a shortened form of **"The goods which have been ordered."**

380. The relative clause misplaced.

> *Don't say:* A boy has a donkey who is in our class.
> *Say:* A boy **who is in our class** has a donkey.

The relative clause must be put immediately after the noun to which it refers.

NOTE. A relative clause that may be omitted is enclosed between commas: as, "My brother George, **who is in another class,** has a new bicycle." A relative clause that cannot be omitted is **not** enclosed within commas: as, "The boy **who spoke to me** is my brother."

381. The conjunction misplaced in a time clause.

> *Don't say:* John when he came the bell had rung.
> *Say:* **When John came** the bell had rung.

The conjunction introducing an adverbial clause of time must be placed at the beginning of a clause.

382. Correlative conjunctions misplaced.

> *Don't say:* He neither speaks English nor French.
> *Say:* He speaks **neither** English **nor** French.

Correlative conjunctions (that is, conjunctions used in pairs, like **"neither . . . nor,"** **"not only . . . but also"**) should be placed before words of the same part of speech.

383. The ordinal numeral misplaced.

> *Don't say:* I have read the two first chapters.
> *Say:* I have read the **first two** chapters.

Ordinal numerals should come before the cardinal. There cannot be two **first** chapters, but only one. Similarly, we must say, "The **last** two (three, etc.)," and not "The two (three, etc.) last."

384. The indefinite article misplaced with **"such"** or **"so."**

> *Don't say:* {I never met a such good man before.
> {I never met a so good man before.
>
> *Say:* {I never met **such a** good man before.
> {I never met **so good a** man before.

The indefinite article **"a"** or **"an"** should come after **"such"** and **"so"**: **"such a good man,"** **"so good a man."**

385. The definite article misplaced with **"half."**

> *Don't say:* The half year is nearly finished.
> *Say:* **Half the year** is nearly finished.

"Half the year" is the shortened form of "half **of** the year."

386. *"The most of"* used instead of **"most of the."**

> *Don't say:* The most of boys are not present.
> *Say:* **Most of the** boys are not present.

The phrase "the most of" is incorrect. Say, **"most of the."**

387. The apostrophe (') misplaced with contractions.

> *Don't write:* Did'nt, has'nt, is'nt, are'nt, etc.
> *Write:* **Didn't, hasn't, isn't, aren't,** etc.

In a contracted word, the apostrophe (') should stand in the place of the omitted letter or letters. The word **"not"** is often contracted and joined to the end of a short word in the form of **"n't"**. Contractions are proper in conversation only.

NOTE. The following contractions are irregular: **"shan't"** (= **shall not**), **"won't"** (= **will not**), **"can't "** (= **cannot**).

(See Exercises 40 and 41 on page 164–165.)

388. Mentioning oneself first.

Don't say: Only I and my brother are present.
Say: Only **my brother and I** are present.

English idiom requires that when a person is speaking of himself and others, he must mention the other person or persons first and leave himself last.

NOTE. But in confessing a fault, the speaker mentions himself first: as, "**I and my brother** broke the window."

Have another look at—

THE CORRECT ORDER OF WORDS

(1) SUBJECT (2) VERB (3) OBJECT

1. The object is usually placed immediately after the verb.

EXAMPLE: I speak English very well.

2. The indirect object usually comes before the direct object *without a preposition*.

EXAMPLE: I gave him the money.

3. An expression of time comes after an expression of place.

EXAMPLE: We stayed there all day.

4. Adverbs of time and degree, such as *always*, *often*, *never*, *nearly*, *hardly*, *scarcely*, are placed before the verb, or between the auxiliary and the verb.

EXAMPLES: I *never* see that man; *or* I have *never* seen that man.

NOTE. But with the verb *to be* the adverb is placed after the verb: as, "He *is* never late."

5. In indirect questions the subject comes first and then the verb.

EXAMPLE: I want to know where they went.

6. In compound verbs with two auxiliaries, *not* is placed after the first one.

EXAMPLE: He could *not* have been there.

7. In the negative infinitive, *not* comes before *to*.

EXAMPLE: I told him *not to go* there.

CHAPTER V

CONFUSED WORDS

PREPOSITIONS OFTEN CONFUSED

389. To and **At.**

(*a*) To.

Don't say: We come at school every morning.
    Say: We **come to** school every morning.

(*b*) At.

Don't say: Someone is standing to the door.
    Say: Someone **is standing at** the door.

"**To**" is used to express motion from one place to another; while "**at**" is used to denote position or rest.

(See Exercise 80 on page 178.)

390. To and **Till.**

(*a*) To.

Don't say: We walked till the river and back.
    Say: We walked **to the river** and back.

(*b*) Till.

Don't say: I shall stay here to next month.
    Say: I shall stay here **till next month.**

"**To**" is used with distance, and "**till**" ("**until**") with time.

COMMON MISTAKES IN ENGLISH

391. At and **In.**

(*a*) At.

Don't say: I spent my holidays in Kyrenia.
     Say: I spent my holidays **at Kyrenia.**

(*b*) In.

Don't say: He lives at London or at New York.
     Say: He lives **in London** or **in New York.**

"**In**" is generally used before the names of countries and large cities, or before the name of the place in which one is at the time of speaking. "**At**" is used before the names of small towns and villages, or in speaking of a distant place.

(See Exercise 81 on page 178.)

392. In and **Into.**

(*a*) In.

Don't say: He spent all the day into his room.
     Say: He spent all the day **in** his room.

(*b*) Into.

Don't say: He came in the room and sat down.
     Say: He came **into** the room and sat down.

"**In**" denotes position or rest inside something; while "**into**" denotes motion or direction towards the inside of something.

NOTE. The preposition "**into**" is always written as one word.

(See Exercise 82 on page 179.)

393. On, At, In. (Time.)

(*a*) On.

Don't say: My uncle will arrive at Saturday.
     Say: My uncle will arrive **on Saturday.**

(*b*) At.

Don't say: I usually get up on five o'clock.

Say: I usually get up **at five o'clock.**

(*c*) In.

Don't say: He takes a walk **at** the afternoon.
   Say: He takes a walk **in the afternoon.**

(1) "**On**" is used with the days of the week or month: as, "**on Friday**," "**on March 25**," "**on New Year's Day**." (2) "**At**" is used with the exact time: as, "**at four o'clock**," "**at dawn**," "**at noon**," "**at sunset**," "**at midnight**." (3) "**In**" is used with a period of time: as, "**in April**," "**in winter**," "**in 1945**," "**in the morning**." But "**at night**" and "**by day**."

(See Exercise 83 on page 179.)

394. For and **At.** (Price.)

(*a*) For.

Don't say: I bought a book at fifty pence.
   Say: I bought a book **for fifty pence.**

(*b*) At.

Don't say: I cannot buy it for such a price.
   Say: I cannot buy it **at such a price.**

"**For**" is used if the actual sum is mentioned: "**at**" is used if the actual sum is not given.

NOTE. But if the weight or measure follows the price, "**at**" may be used with the actual sum: as, "The cloth was sold **at fifty shillings a yard**."

395. Between and **Among.**

(*a*) Between.

Don't say: There was a fight among two boys.
   Say: There was a fight **between two boys.**

(*b*) Among.

Don't say: Divide the apple between you three.
   Say: Divide the apple **among you three.**

91

COMMON MISTAKES IN ENGLISH

"**Between**" is used for two only; while "**among**" is used for more than two.

(See Exercise 85 on page 180.)

396. Beside and Besides.

(*a*) Beside.

Don't say: He was standing just besides me.
    Say: He was standing just **beside** me.

(*b*) Besides.

Don't say: We study French beside English.
    Say: We study French **besides** English.

"**Beside**" means "**by the side of,**" and "**besides**" means "**in addition to.**"

(See Exercise 84 on page 179.)

397. *Except* for **Besides.**

Don't say: I have other books except these.
    Say: I have other books **besides** these (= in addition to these).

NOTE. "**Except**" means leaving out: as, "Everyone was present **except** John."

398. *By* for **With.**

Don't say: The man shot the bird by a gun.
    Say: The man shot the bird **with a gun.**

When we wish to show the means or the instrument with which the action is done, we use "**with.**" "**By**" denotes the doer of the action: as, "The bird was shot **by the man.**"

NOTE. But the following take "**by,**" not "**with**": "by (electric) light," etc., "**by** steam," "**by** hand," "**by** post," "**by** telephone," "**by** one's watch," "**by** the day," "**by** the dozen," "**by** the yard."

399. *From* for **By.**

Don't say: Mary was punished from her father.

Say: Mary **was punished by** her father.

"By" (not **"from"**) should be used after the passive voice to show the doer of the action.

400. *From* for **Of** or **In.**

Don't say: He is the tallest from all the boys.
  Say: He is **the tallest of** all the boys.
  Or: He is **the tallest** boy **in the class.**

Adjectives (or adverbs) in the superlative degree are preceded by **"the"** and followed by **"of"** or **"in."**

401. *For* for **About.**

Don't say: The teacher spoke for bad habits.
  Say: The teacher **spoke about** bad habits.

"For" cannot be used in the sense of **"about."** The chief use of **"for"** is to convey the idea of being in favour of. Therefore, if we say that the teacher "spoke **for** bad habits" it is like saying that he spoke **in favour of** bad habits!

402. *Since* for **For.**

Don't say: He has lived here since two years.
  Say: He has lived here **for two years.**

The preposition **"for"** is placed before words or phrases denoting a period of time: as, **"for three days," "for six weeks," "for two years," "for a few minutes," "for a long time."** It may be used with any tense except the simple present tense.

NOTE. **"For"** is often omitted. We can say, **"I have been here for two years"** or **"I have been here two years."**

403. *From* for **Since.**

Don't say: He has been ill from last Friday.
  Say: He has been ill **since last Friday.**

The preposition **"since"** is placed before words or phrases denoting a point of time: as, **"since Monday," "since yesterday," "since eight o'clock," "since Christmas."** When **"since"** is used, the verb is usually in the present perfect tense, but it may be in the past perfect: as, "I was glad to see Tom. **I had not seen** him **since last Christmas.**"

COMMON MISTAKES IN ENGLISH

NOTE. **"From"** can also denote a point of time, but it must be followed by **"to"** or **"till"**: as, "He works **from** eight o'clock **till** one o'clock without resting."

404. *After* for **In.**

> *Don't say:* I may be able to go after a week.
> *Say:* I may be able to go **in a week.**
> *Or:* I may be able to go **in a week's time.**

When we are speaking of a space of time in the future, we must use **"in,"** and not **"after."** Here **"in"** means **after the end of.**

405. *In* for **Within.**

> *Don't say:* I'll come back in an hour—**if you mean before the end of an hour.**
> *Say:* I'll come back **within an hour.**

"In" means **after the end of;** **"within"** means **before the end of.**

(See Exercises 86 and 87 on page 180–181.)

VERBS OFTEN CONFUSED

406. **Shall** and **Will.**

(*a*) **To express simple futurity:**

In the first person:

> *Don't say:* I will go tomorrow if it is fine.
> *Say:* I **shall** go tomorrow if it is fine.

In the second person:

> *Don't say:* He tells me you shall go tomorrow.
> *Say:* He tells me you **will** go tomorrow.

In the third person:

> *Don't say:* He shall go if he has permission.
> *Say:* He **will** go if he has permission.

Have another look at—

THE USE OF CERTAIN PREPOSITIONS

Prepositions of Place
TO and AT

TO is used for movement from one place to another.

EXAMPLE: I *walk to* school every day.

AT is used to denote position or rest.

EXAMPLE: He is *waiting at* the door.

IN and INTO

IN denotes position or rest inside something.

EXAMPLE: The pencil *is in* the box.

INTO denotes movement towards the inside of something.

EXAMPLE: They *walk into* the room.

Prepositions of Time
AT, ON, IN

AT is used with the exact time.

EXAMPLE: He came *at* 8 *o'clock* in the morning.

ON is used with days and dates.

EXAMPLES: *On Sunday* we go to church. My birthday is *on the third of December*.

IN is used with a period of time.

EXAMPLE: *In summer* the weather is warm.

COMMON MISTAKES IN ENGLISH

(*b*) **To express something more than simple futurity:**

In the first person:

Don't say: I have determined that I shall go.
    Say: I have determined that I **will** go.

In the second person:

Don't say: You will go out if you are good.
    Say: You **shall** go out if you are good.

In the third person:

Don't say: My mind is made up: he will go.
    Say: My mind is made up: he **shall** go.

To form the simple future, we use "**shall**" with the first person and "**will**" with the second and third persons. "**Will**" in the first person denotes resolution or personal determination, and "**shall**" in the second and third persons denotes either a command or a promise.

NOTE. "**Should,**" the past tense of "**shall,**" and "**would,**" the past tense of "**will,**" have the same differences of meaning and use as the present forms "**shall**" and "**will**": as, "I was afraid that I **should** fail"; "I promised that I **would** help him."

(See Exercise 42 on page 165.)

407. Shall and **May.**

Distinguish between:
    (*a*) **May** I shut the door? *and*
    (*b*) **Shall** I shut the door?

"**May** I shut the door?" means that I wish the door closed and I ask your permission to shut it. "**Shall** I shut the door?" means that I want to know whether **you** wish the door closed.

408. Say and **Tell.**

(*a*) Say.

Don't say: {
He told, "I shall go home."
He told that he would go home.

$$Say: \begin{cases} \text{He } \textbf{said}, \text{ "I shall go home."} \\ \text{He } \textbf{said} \text{ that he would go home.} \end{cases}$$

(*b*) Tell.

Don't say: He said to me that he would go home.

Say: He **told me** that he would go home.

"**To say**" is used (1) when referring to a person's actual words, and (2) in indirect speech **if the sentence does not contain an indirect object**. "**To tell**" is used in indirect speech **when the sentence contains an indirect object**. In sentence (*b*) the indirect object is "**me**."

NOTE. Common idioms with "**say**" and "**tell**": (*a*) "To **say** one's prayers," "to **say** grace," "to **say** 'Good morning,'" "to **say** something or nothing," "to **say** no more," "to **say** a good word for," "to **say** so." (*b*) "To **tell** the truth," "to **tell** a lie," "to **tell** a story," "to **tell** the time," "to **tell** a secret," "to **tell** the price," "to **tell** one's fortune," "to **tell** one's name."

(See Exercise 43 on page 165.)

409. Make and **Do.**

(*a*) Make.

Don't say: The carpenter did a large table.

Say: The carpenter **made** a large table.

(*b*) Do.

Don't say: You must make your work carefully.

Say: You must **do** your work carefully.

"**To make**" primarily means to construct or manufacture something; while "**to do**" means to accomplish a thing.

NOTE. Common idioms with "**make**" and "**do**": (*a*) "To **make** a mistake," "to **make** a promise," "to **make** a speech," "to **make** an excuse," "to **make** haste," "to **make** fun of," "to **make** progress," "to **make** a noise," "to **make** an experiment," "to **make** a bed (= to prepare the bed for sleeping upon)." (*b*) "To **do** good," "to **do** evil," "to **do** one's best," "to **do** one a favour," "to **do** wrong," "to **do** a lesson," "to **do** a problem," "to **do** business," "to **do** away with," "to **do** gymnastics," "to **do** exercises."

(See Exercise 44 on page 166.)

410. Lie and Lay.

(*a*) Lie.

Don't say: I am going to lay down for an hour.
     Say: I am going **to lie down** for an hour.

(*b*) Lay.

Don't say: Please lie this letter on the desk.
     Say: Please **lay** this letter on the desk.

"Lie" (= **to rest**) is an intransitive verb and never has an object. "Lay" (= **to put**) is a transitive verb and always requires an object. Their principal parts are **lie, lay, lain,** and **lay, laid, laid.**

NOTE. **Lie, lied, lied** is to tell an untruth: as, "He has **lied** to me." **Lay, laid, laid** means also to produce eggs: as, "The hen has **laid** an egg." (Idiom: **"Lay the table"** or **"Lay the cloth"** is to prepare the table for a meal.)

(See Exercise 45 on page 166.)

411. Sit and Seat.

(*a*) Sit.

Don't say: We seat at a desk to write a letter.
     Say: We **sit** at a desk to write a letter.

(*b*) Seat.

Don't say: He sat the passengers one by one.
     Say: He **seated** the passengers one by one.

"Sit" is best used only as an intransitive verb. "Seat" is a transitive verb and requires an object. Very often the object of "seat" is a reflexive pronoun: as, "He **seated himself** near the fire." The principal parts of the two verbs are: **sit, sat, sat,** and **seat, seated, seated.**

CONFUSED WORDS

NOTE 1. "**Sit**" must not be confused with "**set**." "**Set**," as a transitive verb, means to make a thing sit: as, "**Set** the lamp on the table." "**Set**," as an intransitive verb, means to go down (for sun, moon, or stars): as, "The sun has **set**."

NOTE 2. Common idioms with "**set**": "**To set the table**" (= to put everything ready for the plates of food), "**to set on fire**," "**to set off** (*or* **out**)," "**to set in order**," "**to set a trap**," "**to set a clock**," "**to set a price**," "**to set a price on one's head**," "**to set one's heart on**," "**to set free**," "**to set an example**," "**to set a broken bone**," "**to set to work**" (= to start work).

(See Exercise 46 on page 166.)

412. Rise and Raise.

(*a*) Rise.

Don't say: He raises very early in the morning.
   Say: He **rises** very early in the morning.

(*b*) Raise.

Don't say: Pupils rise their hands too often.
   Say: Pupils **raise** their **hands** too often.

"**Rise**" is an intransitive verb and means to go up, stand up, or get out of bed; it does not require an object. "**Raise**" is a transitive verb and means to lift up **something**. Their principal parts are: **rise, rose, risen**, and **raise, raised, raised**.

NOTE. "**Arise**" is often used for "**rise**," but it is better to use "**arise**" only in the sense of "**begin**": as, "A quarrel (a discussion, an argument, a difficulty, etc.) may **arise**."

(See Exercise 47 on page 167.)

413. Like and Love.

(*a*) Like.

Don't say: Everybody loves polite people.
   Say: Everybody **likes** polite people.

(*b*) Love.

Don't say: Parents like their children.
   Say: Parents **love** their children.

Either verb may be used for persons or things. The only difference between them is one of degree: "to love" is very much stronger than "to like." However, the use of either verb may be correct, as that will often depend upon the person speaking: for example, one person may **like** music, while another one may **love** it.

414. Stay and Remain.

(a) Stay.

Don't say: We remained in a very good hotel.
   Say: We **stayed** in a very good hotel.

(b) Remain.

Don't say: Few figs have stayed on the tree.
   Say: Few figs have **remained** on the tree.

Here, "to stay" means to live for a short time as a guest or a visitor, and **"to remain"** means to be left after part has been taken or destroyed.

NOTE. Either verb may be used when the meaning is to continue in the same place or condition: as, "I shall **stay** (or **remain**) at home till tomorrow."

415. Hanged and Hung.

(a) Hanged.

Don't say: The murderer was caught and hung.
   Say: The murderer was caught and **hanged.**

(b) Hung.

Don't say: We hanged the picture on the wall.
   Say: We **hung** the picture on the wall.

When the reference is to killing a person by hanging, we use the form **"hanged."** In other cases, the form is **"hung."** The principal parts of the two verbs are: **hang, hanged, hanged; hang, hung, hung.**

(See Exercise 51 on page 168.)

416. Wear and **Put on.**

(*a*) Wear.

Don't say: This man always puts on black shoes.
Say: This man always **wears** black shoes.

(*b*) Put on.

Don't say: I wear my clothes in the morning.
Say: I **put on** my clothes in the morning.

"Wear" means to have upon the body as a garment or as an ornament. "**To put on**" denotes a simple act.

NOTE. "**To dress**" has nearly the same meaning as "**to put on**," but the object of "**dress**" is a person and not a thing: as, "He **dressed himself** and went out"; "The mother **dressed** her **baby**."

(See Exercise 48 on page 167.)

417. Tear and **Tear up.**

(*a*) Tear.

Don't say: John tore up his coat on a nail.
Say: John **tore** his coat on a nail.

(*b*) Tear up.

Don't say: He was angry and tore the letter.
Say: He was angry and **tore up** the letter.

"**To tear**" means to divide along a straight or irregular line, sometimes by accident; "**to tear up**" means to destroy by tearing to pieces.

NOTE. The word "**up**" is often used with verbs to express the idea of greater completeness: as, *burn up, drink up, dry up, cut up, eat up, shut up, use up.*

418. Grow and **Grow up.**

(*a*) Grow.

Don't say: Babies grow up very quickly.
Say: Babies **grow** very quickly.

COMMON MISTAKES IN ENGLISH

(*b*) Grow up.

Don't say: When I grow I shall be a doctor.
Say: When I **grow up** I shall be a doctor.

"**To grow**" means to become bigger; "**to grow up**" means to become a man (or a woman).

NOTE. Other meanings of "**grow**": (1) to cultivate: as, "Rice **grows** in Egypt"; (2) to cause to grow: as, "We **grow** flowers in our garden"; (3) to allow to grow: as, "He **grew** a beard"; (4) to become: as, "The nights **grow** cold in winter."

419. Pick and Pick up.

(*a*) Pick.

Don't say: We picked up flowers in the garden.
Say: We **picked** flowers in the garden.

(*b*) Pick up.

Don't say: The naughty boy picked a stone.
Say: The naughty boy **picked up** a stone.

"**To pick fruit or flowers**" means to pull them away with the fingers; "**to pick up**" means to lift up from the ground.

420. Deal with and Deal in.

(*a*) Deal with.

Don't say: This book deals in common errors.
Say: This book **deals with** common errors.

(*b*) Deal in.

Don't say: A bookseller deals with books.
Say: A bookseller **deals in** books.

"**To deal with**" means to have to do with; "**to deal in**" means to buy and sell.

NOTE. "**To deal with**" also means (1) to do business with: as, "I will not **deal with** that shopkeeper again"; (2) to arrange a matter: as, "The headmaster will **deal with** that question."

421. Interfere with and **Interfere in.**

(a) Interfere with.

Don't say: The noise interferes in my work.
　　Say: The noise **interferes with** my work.

(b) Interfere in.

Don't say: I never interfere with his affairs.
　　Say: I never **interfere in** his affairs.

"**To interfere with**" means to be an obstacle to; "**to interfere in**" means to take part in other people's affairs without any right.

422. Borrow and **Lend.**

(a) Borrow.

Don't say: I want to lend a book from you.
　　Say: I want to **borrow** a book from you.

(b) Lend.

Don't say: Will you please borrow me a book?
　　Say: Will you please **lend** me a book?

"**To borrow**" is to get something from someone, and "**to lend**" is to give something to someone.

(See Exercise 52 on page 168.)

423. Steal and **Rob.**

(a) Steal.

Don't say: Someone has robbed all his money.
　　Say: Someone has **stolen** all his **money.**

(b) Rob.

Don't say: Some men stole a bank last night.
　　Say: Some men **robbed a bank** last night.

The object of "**steal**" is the thing taken by the thief, such as money, a watch, a bicycle, etc.; while the object of "**rob**" is the person or place from whom (or which) the thing is taken, such as a man, a house, or a bank.

(See Exercise 53 on page 168.)

424. Revenge and Avenge.

(*a*) Revenge.

Don't say: I avenged myself for the insult.
 Say: I **revenged** myself for the insult.

(*b*) Avenge.

Don't say: He now revenged his son's murder.
 Say: He now **avenged** his son's murder.

"To revenge oneself" is to punish for a wrong done to oneself: while "to avenge" is to punish on behalf of another, usually the innocent or weak.

NOTE. The noun "revenge" is commonly used in the expressions "to take revenge on" and "to get or have one's revenge": as, "He took revenge on the boy who had struck him"; "He could not rest until he had his revenge."

425. Convince and Persuade.

(*a*) Convince.

Don't say: I am now persuaded of his honesty.
 Say: I am now **convinced** of his honesty.

(*b*) Persuade.

Don't say: We could not convince him to play.
 Say: We could not **persuade** him to play.

"To convince" is to make a person believe; while "to persuade" means to get a person to do something.

NOTE. Care must be taken not to confuse "persuade" with "pursued," the past tense of "pursue" (= to follow).

426. Refuse and Deny.

(*a*) Refuse.

Don't say: The boy denied to take the money.
 Say: The boy **refused** to take the money.

(*b*) Deny.

Don't say: John refused that he had done it.

CONFUSED WORDS

Say: John **denied** that he had done it.

"To refuse" means not to take what is offered or not to do what one is asked to do; **"to deny"** means to answer in the negative or to say that a statement is not true.

(See Exercise 54 on page 169.)

427. Discover and Invent.

(*a*) Discover.

Don't say: America was invented by Columbus.
    Say: America was **discovered** by Columbus.

(*b*) Invent.

Don't say: Edison discovered the gramophone.
    Say: Edison **invented** the gramophone.

"To discover" is to find that which existed before but was unknown, and **"to invent"** is to make that which did not exist before.

428. Take place and Take part.

(*a*) Take place.

Don't say: The meeting will take part soon.
    Say: The meeting will **take place** soon.

(*b*) Take part.

Don't say: I shall take place in the meeting.
    Say: I shall **take part** in the meeting.

"To take place" means to happen or to be held; while **"to take part"** means to have a share in a thing.

429. Made of and Made from.

(*a*) Made of.

Don't say: Tables are usually made from wood.
    Say: Tables are usually **made of wood.**

(*b*) Made from.

Don't say: Bread is usually made of wheat.
Say: Bread is usually **made from wheat**.

"**Made of**" is used if the material of which the thing is made can still be seen: and "**made from**" if the material can no longer be seen.

430. *Let* for **Rent**.

Don't say: I let the house from Mr. Jones.
Say: I **rented** the house from Mr. Jones.

A landlord (= the owner) **lets** or **rents** a house, etc., but a tenant (= a person paying rent) **rents** a house, etc.—only the owner can **let** a house, etc.

NOTE. "**To hire**" is to pay for the use of something *for a short time*: as, **to hire** a horse, a bicycle, a car, a rowing-boat, or a concert hall for one evening. "**To hire out**" is to allow others to use something on payment: as, "He **hires out** bicycles by the hour."

431. *Win* for **Earn**.

Don't say: He wins his living by hard work.
Say: He **earns** his living by hard work.

"**To earn**" means to receive in return for work; "**to win**" is to obtain as a result of fighting, competition, gambling, etc.

NOTE. The verb "**to gain**" may be used with either meaning: **to gain one's living** or **to gain a victory, a prize,** etc.

432. *Substitute* for **Replace**.

Don't say: They substituted gold by paper-money.
Say: They **replaced** gold **by** paper-money.

We **replace** one thing **by** another, but we **substitute** one thing **for** another: as, "They **substituted** paper-money **for** gold."

433. *Correct* for **Repair** or **Mend**.

Don't say: Some men are correcting the road.
Say: Some men are **repairing** the road.

CONFUSED WORDS

"To correct" is to make something right: **to correct** mistakes, a composition, a translation, one's pronunciation, etc.; **"to repair"** or **"to mend"** is to put in good condition after being damaged: **to repair** or **mend** a road, clothes, shoes, etc.

NOTE. **"To repair a watch"** is to put it in good condition again, but **"to correct a watch"** is to set it by the right time.

434. *Dust* for **Cover with dust.**

Don't say: A sandstorm dusted our clothes.

Say: A sandstorm **covered** our clothes **with dust.**

"To dust" does not mean to cover with dust, but to remove dust from: as, "After sweeping, she **dusted** the furniture."

435. *Please* for **Ask** or **Thank.**

Don't say: I pleased him to do me a favour;

or: I pleased him for his fine present.

Say: I **asked** him to do me a favour;

and: I **thanked** him for his fine present.

"To please" means to give pleasure to: as, "I worked hard to **please** my teacher."

436. *Can* for **May.**

Don't say: Sir, can I go home to get my book?

Say: Sir, **may** I go home to get my book?

"Can" means **to be able**; **"may"** means **to have permission.**

NOTE. In ordinary conversation **"can"** also has the meaning of permission: as, "You **can** (= may) go now."

(See Exercise 55 on page 169.)

437. *Could* for **Was able to.**

Don't say: Because he worked hard he could finish the job in time.

Say: Because he worked hard he **was able to** finish the job in time.

If the meaning is *managed to* or *succeeded in doing*, **"was able to,"** and not **"could,"** should be used.

438. *Learn* for **Teach.**

> *Don't say:* He learned us how to play hockey.
> *Say:* He **taught** us how to play hockey.

"Teach" means to give instruction; **"learn"** means to receive instruction: as, "He **taught** me English, and I **learned** it quickly."

(See Exercise 56 on page 169.)

439. *Win* for **Beat.**

> *Don't say:* We have always won your team.
> *Say:* We have always **beaten** your team.

"To win" is to gain something for which you have tried; **"to beat"** is to overcome an opponent: as, "The girls **beat** the boys, and so **won** the prize."

REMEMBER the principal parts of each verb: **beat, beat, beaten,** and **win, won, won.**

(See Exercise 57 on page 169.)

440. *Accept* for **Agree.**

> *Don't say:* The teacher accepted to go with us.
> *Say:* The teacher **agreed** to go with us.

"Accept" means to take what is offered: as, "I **accepted** his invitation." **"Agree"** means to do what one is asked to do: as, "He **agreed to play."** **"Accept"** cannot be followed by an infinitive.

NOTE. We agree **with** a person, but **to** a thing: as, "I agree **with** Mr. A., but I cannot **agree to** this plan."

441. *Leave* for **Let.**

> *Don't say:* He did not leave me to get my book.
> *Say:* He did not **let** me get my book.

"Let" means to allow. **"Leave"** means to abandon or to go away from: as, "Do you **leave** your books in school?"

(See also §§ 447 and 459.)

CONFUSED WORDS

442. *Bring* for **Take.**

> *Don't say:* I shall bring it to England with me.
> *Say:* I shall **take** it to England with me.

When you go out with something, you **take** it; if you come in with something, then you **bring** it.

NOTE. "**To fetch**" means to go and come back with something; as, "Please **fetch** me a glass of water" (= go and come back with a glass of water).

443. *Drown* for **Sink.**

> *Don't say:* The ship was drowned in the ocean.
> *Say:* The ship was **sunk** in the ocean.

"**To be drowned**" is used only of living things, and means to die in water; "**to sink**" is used of persons or things, and means to go down to the bottom of water.

444. *See* for **Look.**

> *Don't say:* He was seeing out of the window.
> *Say:* He was **looking** out of the window.

"**To see**" is to notice with the eyes, but "**to look**" is to direct the eyes in order to see: as, "I **looked** up and **saw** the aeroplane."

(See Exercise 58 on page 169.)

445. *Hear* for **Listen.**

> *Don't say:* I was hearing her sweet song.
> *Say:* I was **listening to** her sweet song.

"**To listen**" implies attention, "**to hear**" does not: as, "I **heard** them talking but I did not **listen to** what they said." "**To listen**" also means to accept advice: as, "He **listens to** his parents."

(See Exercise 59 on page 170.)

446. *Remember* for **Remind.**

> *Don't say:* Please remember me to give it back.
> *Say:* Please **remind** me to give it back.

"**To remember**" is to have in mind: as, "I **remember** what you told me." "**To remind**" is to make another person remember something.

447. *Leave* for **Let go.**

Don't say: Leave the other end of the string.
Say: **Let go of** the other end of the string.

"**Leave**" cannot be used in the sense of "**let go**" (= give up one's hold).

448. *Sleep* for **Go to Bed.**

Don't say: I shall sleep early tonight.
Say: I shall **go to bed** early tonight.

"**To go to bed**" denotes the act of lying down on a bed in preparation for going to sleep. Thus we can say that a person "**went to bed**" at nine o'clock, but that he did not "**sleep**" until eleven o'clock. Then he "**slept**" soundly.

NOTE. "**Go to sleep**" means to fall asleep: as, "He **went to sleep** while he was in the cinema."

449. *To be found* for **To be.**

Don't say: The man was found in his office.
Say: The man **was** in his office.

In English, the verb "**to be found**" generally means "**to be discovered**": as, "Diamonds **are found** in Africa and in India." Therefore, "**He was found in his office**" would suggest that the man had hidden himself in his office and was later **discovered.**

450. *To be with* for **To have.**

Don't say: My English book is with my brother.
Say: **My brother has my English book.**

Avoid using "**to be with**" in the sense of "**to have.**" "**To be with**" means to be together or in company of: as, "He **is with** his parents."

CONFUSED WORDS

451. *Take* for **Get** (or **Receive**).

> *Don't say:* He took a high mark in English.
> *Say:* He **got** a high mark in English.
> *Or:* He **received** a high mark in English.

"To take" means to obtain something intentionally or by force: as, "I **took** a book from the library"; "The army **took** the city." **"To get"** or **"to receive"** means to obtain something which is given one, such as a gift, a letter, money, or a mark in the examination.

452. *Like* for **Want**, etc.

> *Don't say:* Do you like to see my collection?
> *Say:* Do you **want** to see my collection?

"Do you like to do something?" means do you enjoy doing it as a habitual action. **"Do you want to do something?"** means do you wish to do it **now**.

NOTE. But **"I should like"** means I want: as, **"I should like** (= I want) to play tennis today"; **"Would you like** (= do you **want**) to go for a walk with me?"

(See Exercise 60 on page 170.)

453. *I don't have* for **I haven't.**

> *Don't say:* I don't have time to see you today.
> *Say:* **I haven't** time to see you today.

"I don't have" is used for things occurring habitually: as, **"I don't have** fruit for breakfast." **"I haven't"** is used to refer to particular occasions, and means I haven't something **now**.

454. *Know* for **Learn,** etc.

> *Don't say:* He went to school to know English.
> *Say:* He went to school to **learn** English.

"Know" is used when **"learning"** is finished: as, "He **knows** how to swim." Similarly, avoid using **"know"** with the meaning of **"find out"** or **"realize."**

COMMON MISTAKES IN ENGLISH

455. *Read* for **Study.**

> *Don't say:* He is reading algebra in his room.
> *Say:* He is **studying** algebra in his room.

"To study" means to try to learn; "to read" does not imply any effort. Thus, a student "**studies**" English, mathematics, history, and other subjects; he "**reads**" a story, a letter, or a newspaper. But "He is **reading** for a degree in Arts" is correct.

(See Exercise 61 on page 170.)

456. *Learn* for **Study.**

> *Don't say:* He is learning at Gordon College.
> *Say:* He is **studying** at Gordon College.

The expression "**I learn at (Gordon College,**" etc.) is incorrect. Say "**I study at (Gordon College,**" etc.) or "**I am a student of (Gordon College,**" etc.).

457. *Take* for **Buy.**

> *Don't say:* I went to the baker's to take bread.
> *Say:* I went to the baker's to **buy** bread.

Never use "**take**" in the sense of "**buy.**"

458. *Take out* for **Take off.**

> *Don't say:* He took out his hat and overcoat.
> *Say:* He **took off** his hat and overcoat.

The opposite of "**put on**" is "**take off,**" and not "**take out.**"

459. *Leave* for **Give up,** etc.

> *Don't say:* I have now left football.
> *Say:* I have now **given up** football.
> *Or:* I have now **stopped** playing football.

"**Leave**" should never be used in the meaning of "**give up,**" or "**stop**" something.

(For §§ 441, 447 and 459 see Exercise 49 on page 167.)

CONFUSED WORDS

460. *Sympathize* for **Like**.

> *Don't say:* I don't sympathize him very much.
> *Say:* I don't **like** him very much.

"Sympathize" is not synonymous with "like." "To sympathize with" means to share some feeling (usually of sorrow) with another person: as, "I **sympathize with** you in your sorrow."

461. *Put* for **Keep**.

> *Don't say:* Do you put your money in the bank?
> *Say:* Do you **keep** your money in the bank?

It is better to use "keep" of a more or less permanent resting-place, and "put" of a temporary one.

462. *Care for* for **Take care of**.

> *Don't say:* He doesn't care for his money.
> *Say:* He doesn't **take care of** his money.

"Care for" cannot be used in the sense of "take care of." "To care for" means to like: as, "I don't **care for** the book" (= "I don't like the book").

NOTE. Avoid also such expressions as: (1) "He does not care for my advice"; (2) "He does not care for his work"; (3) "He took no care of him"; (4) "No one cared for him during his illness." Say: (1) **"He pays no attention to my advice"**; (2) **"He takes no care over his work"**; (3) **"He took no notice of him"**; (4) **"No one took care of him during his illness."**

463. *Let* for **Make** (= **to force**).

> *Don't say:* He let him write it fifty times.
> *Say:* He **made** him write it fifty times.

"Let" cannot be used in the sense of "make", meaning "to force."

464. *Flown* for **Flowed**.

> *Don't say:* The river has flown over its banks.
> *Say:* The river has **flowed** over its banks.

"Flown" is the past participle of **"fly"**; the past participle of **"flow"** (= to move as water) is **"flowed."** The principal parts of the two verbs are: **fly, flew, flown—flow, flowed, flowed.**

NOTE. **"Flee, fled, fled"** means to run away: as, "We **flee** from danger." **"Float, floated, floated"** means to rest or move on the surface of water or other liquid: as, "Ships **float** on the water."

(See Exercise 50 on page 168.)

465. *Fall* for **Fell.**

> *Don't say:* John fall down and broke his leg.
> *Say:* John **fell** down and broke his leg.

The past tense of this verb is **"fell,"** not **"fall."** Its principal parts are: **fall, fell, fallen.**

NOTE. **"Fell, felled, felled"** means to knock or cut down: as, "The wood-cutter **felled** a large tree."

(See Exercise 62 on page 170.)

466. *Found* for **Find.**

> *Don't say:* He tried to found his lost book.
> *Say:* He tried **to find** his lost book.

"To find" is a very common verb meaning to get back a thing lost. Its principal parts are: *find, found, found.*

NOTE. There is, however, another verb **"to found,"** meaning to establish: as, "He **founded** the school fifty years ago."

(See also Exercise 63 on page 171.)

ADVERBS OFTEN CONFUSED

467. Very and **Too.**

(*a*) Very.

> *Don't say:* Here it is too hot in the summer.
> *Say:* Here it is **very** hot in the summer.

CONFUSED WORDS

(*b*) Too

Don't say: It is now very hot to play football.
   Say: It is now **too** hot to play football.

"Very" simply makes the adjective or adverb stronger. "Too" means more than enough, or so much that something else happens as a result. The sentence **"It is too hot in the summer"** is not complete: "**too** hot for what?"—"**Too** hot to play football," but the incompleted phrase is used sometimes in spoken English.

(See Exercise 71 on page 174.)

468. Very and **Much.**

(*a*) Very.

Don't say: { He is a much strong man.
{ It is a much interesting book.

   Say: { He is a **very strong** man.
{ It is a **very interesting** book.

(*b*) Much.

Don't say: { He is very stronger than I am.
{ I am very obliged to my friend.

   Say: { He is **much** stronger than I am.
{ I am **much** obliged to my friend.

"Very" is used with adjectives and adverbs in the positive degree, and with present participles used as adjectives (like "**interesting**"). "**Much**" is used with adjectives and adverbs in the comparative degree, and with past participles.

NOTE. A few past participles that are used almost in the sense of adjectives may take "**very**" before them: as, "I am **very** pleased (= glad) to see you"; "I am **very** tired"; "The accommodation is **very** limited." But: "I was **much** (not **very**) afraid of falling."

(See Exercise 72 on page 175.)

469. *Too much* for **Very much.**

Don't say: { He likes the cinema too much.
He is too much stronger than I am.
I was too much astonished at the news.

Say: { He likes the cinema **very much.**
He is **very much** stronger than I am.
I was **very much** astonished at the news.

"Very much" is used instead of "much" for greater emphasis.
"Too much" denotes an excessive quantity or degree: as, "He
ate **too much**, and became ill."

NOTE. "Much" and "very much" cannot be used with certain
verbs, like "work," "try," "rain," "think," "to be hurt," "to be
injured." Thus we say: "He works very **hard**"; "He tried very
hard"; "It is raining **hard**"; "He thinks **deeply**"; "He was
badly hurt"; "He was **seriously** injured."

(See Exercise 73 on page 175.)

470. *Before* for **Ago.**

Don't say: I saw your friend before two weeks.
Say: I saw your friend **two weeks ago.**

We use "ago" in counting from the time of speaking to a point
in the past: as, "**half an hour ago**," "**three days ago**," "**four
months ago**," "**five years ago**," "**a long time ago.**" We use
"before" in counting from a distant to a nearer point in the
past: as, "Napoleon died in 1821; he had lost the battle of
Waterloo six years **before.**"

NOTE. When "ago" is used, the verb is always in the past
tense: as, "He **came** five minutes ago."

471. *Hardly* for **Hard.**

Don't say: They said that he was hit hardly.
Say: They said that he was hit **hard.**

"Hard" means **severely.** "Hardly" means **not quite** or **scarcely**:
as, "The baby can **hardly** walk."

(See Exercise 74 on page 175.)

116

CONFUSED WORDS

472. *So* for **Very.**

> *Don't say:* I hear that he is not so rich.
> *Say:* I hear that he is not **very** rich.

"So" cannot be used in the sense of "**very.**" The expression "He is not so rich" implies a comparison: as, "He is not **so** rich **as** you are."

473. *By and by* for **Gradually.**

> *Don't say:* It is learning to walk by and by.
> *Say:* It is **gradually** learning to walk.

"**Gradually**" means slowly or little by little; "**by and by**" means soon or after a little while: as, "**By and by** the school year will be over."

474. *Just now* for **Presently,** etc.

> *Don't say:* The messenger will arrive just now.
> *Say:* The messenger will arrive **presently.**

If we are speaking of a near and immediate future time, we must use "**presently,**" "**immediately,**" or "**soon.**" "**Just now**" refers to present or past time, and not to future time: as, "He is not at home **just now** (= at this moment)"; "He left **just now** (= a little time ago)."

475. *Presently* for **At present.**

> *Don't say:* His uncle is presently in London.
> *Say:* His uncle is **at present** in London.

"**At present**" and "**presently**" are not synonymous. "**At present**" means **now,** but "**presently**" means **soon:** as, "He will come back **presently** (= soon)."

476. *Scarcely* for **Rarely.**

> *Don't say:* He scarcely comes to see me now.
> *Say:* He **rarely** comes to see me now.

"**Scarcely**" is not synonymous with "**rarely.**" "**Rarely**" means **not often**; "**scarcely**" means **not quite:** as, "I had **scarcely** finished when he came."

117

477. *Lately* for **Late.**

> *Don't say:* Last night I went to bed lately.
> *Say:* Last night I went to bed **late.**

The opposite of **"early"** is **"late,"** not **"lately."** **"Lately"** means **in recent times**: as, "I haven't been there **lately**."

ADJECTIVES OFTEN CONFUSED

478. Many and **Much.**

(*a*) Many.

> *Don't say:* My brother hasn't much books.
> *Say:* My brother hasn't **many books.**

(*b*) Much.

> *Don't say:* Is there many dust in the field?
> *Say:* Is there **much dust** in the field?

"Many" is used with plural nouns: as, **many** books *or* **many** boys; **"much"** is used with singular nouns that have no plural: as, **much** water *or* **much** bread.

NOTE. In affirmative sentences **many** and **much** are generally replaced by **a lot (of), a great deal (of), plenty (of), a good deal (of), a good many (of), a great number (of), a large quantity (of),** etc.

(See Exercise 10 on page 152.)

479. Few and **A Few.**

(*a*) Few.

> *Don't say:* Although the question was easy, a few boys were able to answer it.
> *Say:* Although the question was easy, **few** boys were able to answer it.

(*b*) A few.

Don't say: Although the question was difficult, few boys were able to answer it.

Say: Although the question was difficult, **a few** boys were able to answer it.

"Few" means **not many** and emphasizes the smallness of the number. It is distinguished from "a few," which means **at least some.**

480. Little and A little.

(*a*) Little.

Don't say: He slept a little and felt no better.
Say: He slept **little** and felt no better.

(*b*) A little.

Don't say: He slept little and felt better.
Say: He slept **a little** and felt better.

"Little" means **not much** and emphasizes the smallness of the amount. It is distinguished from "a little" which means **at least some.**

(For §§ 479–480 see Exercise 11 on page 153.)

481. Each and Every.

(*a*) Each.

Don't say: Every one of the two boys was wrong.
Say: **Each** one of the two boys was wrong.

(*b*) Every.

Don't say: She read each book of the library.
Say: She read **every** book of the library.

"Each" is used for one of two or more things, taken **one by one.** "Every" is never used for two, but always for more than two things, taken **as a group.** "Each" is thus more individual and specific, but "every" is the more emphatic word.

NOTE. **"Each"** and **"every"** are always singular: as, **"Each** (or **every**) one of the twenty boys **has** a book."

482. His and Her.

(a) His.

Don't say: John visits her aunt every Sunday.
Say: **John** visits **his** aunt every Sunday.

(b) Her.

Don't say: Ann visits his uncle every Sunday.
Say: **Ann** visits **her** uncle every Sunday.

In English, possessive adjectives (and pronouns) agree with the person **who possesses**, and not with the person or thing possessed. When the possessor is masculine, use **"his,"** and when the possessor is feminine, use **"her."**

(See Exercise 14 on page 154.)

483. Older (oldest) and Elder (eldest).

(a) Older, Oldest.

Don't say: {This boy is elder than that one.
{This boy is the eldest of all.
Say: {This boy is **older** than that one.
{This boy is the **oldest** of all.

(b) Elder, Eldest.

Don't say: {My older brother is called John.
{My oldest brother is not here.
Say: {My **elder** brother is called John.
{My **eldest** brother is not here.

"Older" and **"oldest"** are applied to both persons and things; while **"elder"** and **"eldest"** are applied to persons only, and most frequently to related persons. (Warning: **"Elder"** cannot be followed by **"than"**: as, "Jane is **older** (not **elder**) than her sister.")

CONFUSED WORDS

484. Interesting and Interested.

(*a*) Interesting.

Don't say: I have read an interested story.
Say: I have read an **interesting** story.

(*b*) Interested.

Don't say: Are you interesting in your work?
Say: Are you **interested** in your work?

"Interesting" refers to the thing which arouses interest; while **"interested"** refers to the person who takes an interest in the thing.

(See Exercise 15 on page 154.)

485. Wounded and Injured or Hurt.

(*a*) Wounded.

Don't say: Thousands were injured in the war.
Say: Thousands were **wounded** in the war.

(*b*) Injured *or* Hurt.

Don't say: He was wounded in a motor accident.
Say: He was **injured** in a motor accident.

People are **injured** or **hurt** as a result of an accident, and **wounded** in battle or in war. (The nouns are **injury** and **wound**.)

486. Farther and Further.

(*a*) Farther.

Don't say: New York is further than London.
Say: New York is **farther** than London.

(*b*) Further.

Don't say: I shall get farther information.
Say: I shall get **further** information.

The distinction often made between the two words is that **"farther"** means **more distant**, and **"further"** means **additional**. However, current usage prefers **"further"** in all meanings.

121

COMMON MISTAKES IN ENGLISH

487. *A* for **An.**

> *Don't say:* A animal; a orange; a hour.
> *Say:* **An** animal; **an** orange; **an** hour.

"**An**" is used instead of "**a**" before a vowel or a silent "**h**" (as in "**hour**," "**heir**," "**honest**"). Before a long "**u**" or a syllable having the sound of "**you**," we use "**a**" (not "**an**"); as, "**a** union," "**a** European" (but "**an uncle**").

488. *One* for **A(n).**

> *Don't say:* He found one ring in the street.
> *Say:* He found **a** ring in the street.

The numeral "**one**" should not be used instead of the indefinite article "**a**" or "**an**." "**One**" is to be used only where the number is emphatic: as, "He gave me **one** book instead of two."

489. *Some* for **Any.**

> *Don't say:* { Have you some lessons to prepare?
> { I haven't some lessons to prepare.
> *Say:* { Have you **any** lessons to prepare?
> { I haven't **any** lessons to prepare.

"**Any**" (not "**some**") must be used in interrogative and negative sentences.

NOTE. "**Some**" is generally used in affirmative sentences, or in interrogative sentences expecting an affirmative answer: as, "Will you bring me **some** water?"

(See Exercise 13 on page 153.)

490. *Less* for **Fewer.**

> *Don't say:* They have less books than I have.
> *Say:* They have **fewer** books than I have.

"**Less**" denotes amount, quantity, value, or degree; "**fewer**" denotes number. Thus, we may have "**less** water," "**less** food," "**less** money," "**less** education"; but "**fewer** books," "**fewer** letters," "**fewer** friends."

NOTE. We say "**less** than (five, six, etc.) pounds" because the pounds are considered as a sum of money and not as a number of coins.

491. *This* for **That**.

>*Don't say:* Look at this dog across the street.
>*Say:* Look at **that** dog across the street.

You cannot use **"this"** unless the object is being touched by you. **"That"** must be used to point out something distant, and the correct answer to **"What is this?"** is always **"That is a . . ."**

492. *Latter* for **Later**.

>*Don't say:* She came to school latter than I.
>*Say:* She came to school **later** than I.

"Later" refers to time. **"Latter"** refers to order and means the second of two things just mentioned: as, "Alexandria and Cairo are large cities; the **latter** has a population of over a million." The opposite of **"latter"** is **"former."**

493. *Last* for **Latter**.

>*Don't say:* Scott and Dickens are both excellent writers, but I prefer the last.
>*Say:* Scott and Dickens are both excellent writers, but I prefer the **latter**.

"The latter" means the second of two persons or things which have been mentioned; **"the last"** refers to a series of more than two.

494. *Last* for **Latest**.

>*Don't say:* What is the last news of the war?
>*Say:* What is the **latest** news of the war?

"Latest" is the last up to the present. **"Last"** is the final one: as, "**Z** is the **last** letter of the alphabet."

495. *Small, Big* for **Young, Old**.

>*Don't say:* { I am two years smaller than you.
> { He is three years bigger than I.
>*Say:* { I am two years **younger** than you.
> { He is three years **older** than I.

If reference is to age, say **"young"** or **"old." "Small"** and **"big"** usually refer to size: as, "He is **big** (or **small**) for his age."

NOTE. **"Great"** refers to the importance of a person or thing; as, "Napoleon was a **great** man"; "Homer's *Iliad* is a **great** book." **"Great"** is also used with words like **"distance,"** **"height,"** **"length,"** **"depth"**: as, "There is a **great** distance between the earth and the moon."

496. *High* for **Tall.**

Don't say: My elder brother is six feet high.
Say: My elder brother is six feet **tall.**

"Tall" is generally used of persons, and is the opposite of **"short." "High"** is used of trees, buildings, or mountains, and is the opposite of **"low."**

497. *Lovely* for **Beloved.**

Don't say: Joseph was Jacob's lovely son.
Say: Joseph was Jacob's **beloved** son.

We should say **"beloved"** if we mean **much loved. "Lovely"** means **beautiful**: as, a **lovely** woman, a **lovely** day, etc.

NOTE. Care must also be taken not to confuse **"lovely"** with **"favourite"** (= most liked). Say: "Who is your **favourite** English writer?" *or* "What is your **favourite** game?"

498. *Beautiful* for **Handsome** or **Good-looking.**

Don't say: He has grown into a beautiful youth.
Say: He has grown into a **handsome** youth.

We usually say that a man is **handsome** or **good-looking**, and that a woman is **beautiful** or **pretty.**

499. *Sick* for **Ill.**

Don't say: He has been sick for over a year.
Say: He has been **ill** for over a year.

"To be ill" means to be in bad health. **"To be sick"** generally means to be inclined to vomit or to be temporarily indisposed: as, "The smell made me **sick.**"

NOTE. **"Sick"** can also be used before a noun or as a noun in the plural: as, "The **sick** man is lying in bed"; "We visit the **sick**." "**Ill**" could not be used in this way.

(See Exercise 12 on page 153.)

500. *Clear* for **Clean.**

> *Don't say:* You should keep your hands clear.
> *Say:* You should keep your hands **clean.**

"**Clean**" is the opposite of "**dirty**." "**Clear**" means transparent or unclouded: as, "**clear** water," "a **clear** sky."

501. *Angry* for **Sorry.**

> *Don't say:* I was angry to hear of his death.
> *Say:* I was **sorry** to hear of his death.

"**Sorry**" is the opposite of "**glad.**" "**Angry**" means **annoyed** or **enraged**: as, "He was **angry** when a boy hit him in the face."

502. *Nervous* for **Angry.**

> *Don't say:* Our teacher is very nervous today.
> *Say:* Our teacher is very **angry** today.

"**Nervous**" denotes the habit of being easily excited or frightened. This word cannot be used in the sense of "**angry**," which denotes only a temporary state.

(See also Exercise 16 on page 154.)

NOUNS OFTEN CONFUSED

503. House and **Home.**

(*a*) House.

> *Don't say:* Many new homes have been built.
> *Say:* Many new **houses** have been built.

(*b*) Home.

> *Don't say:* You should go to your house now.
> *Say:* You should go **home** now.

Take care not to say "**my house**," "**his house**," or "**your house**" when you should rather say "**home**." A "**house**" is any building

125

COMMON MISTAKES IN ENGLISH

used for dwelling in, and **"home"** is the particular house in which one is living.

NOTE. **"Home"** may also denote one's own country. When an Englishman says "I am going **home** this summer" he means going to England.

(See Exercise 4 on page 150.)

504. Street and Road.

(*a*) Street.

Don't say: The roads of the town are narrow.
Say: The **streets** of the town are narrow.

(*b*) Road.

Don't say: Which is the street to the village?
Say: Which is the **road** to the village?

A **"street"** is a way in a town or village with buildings on the sides; a **"road"** usually denotes a way leading from one town or village to another.

NOTE. We say **"on** the road" or **"on** the way," but **"in** the street."

(See Exercise 5 on page 150.)

505. Story and History.

(*a*) Story.

Don't say: She told me an interesting history.
Say: She told me an interesting **story.**

(*b*) History.

Don't say: We study the story of the Romans.
Say: We study the **history** of the Romans.

A **"story"** is an account of events which may or may not be true; **"history"** is a systematic record of past events.

126

CONFUSED WORDS

506. Habit and **Custom.**

(*a*) Habit.

Don't say: Telling lies is a very bad custom.
Say: Telling lies is a very bad **habit.**

(*b*) Custom.

Don't say: The Chinese have strange habits.
Say: The Chinese have strange **customs.**

A "**habit**" belongs to the individual, but a "**custom**" belongs to a society or country.

(See Exercise 6 on page 151.)

507. Cause and **Reason.**

(*a*) Cause.

Don't say: What is the reason of a sandstorm?
Say: What is the **cause** of a sandstorm?

(*b*) Reason.

Don't say: You have a good cause for coming.
Say: You have a good **reason** for coming.

A "**cause**" is that which produces a result; a "**reason**" is that which explains or justifies a result.

508. Scene and **Scenery.**

(*a*) Scene.

Don't say: The scenery is of a beautiful lake.
Say: The **scene** is of a beautiful lake.

(*b*) Scenery.

Don't say: The scene in Cyprus is beautiful.
Say: The **scenery** in Cyprus is beautiful.

A "**scene**" refers to one particular place, while "**scenery**" refers to the general appearance of the country. "**Scenery**" cannot be used in the plural.

COMMON MISTAKES IN ENGLISH

509. Centre and Middle.

(a) Centre.

Don't say: Can you find the middle of a table?
    Say: Can you find the **centre** of a table?

(b) Middle.

Don't say: He was in the centre of the street.
    Say: He was in the **middle** of the street.

"Centre" is a definite point, while "middle" is the indefinite space around or near the "centre."

510. Shade and Shadow.

(a) Shade.

Don't say: That large tree makes a nice shadow.
    Say: That large tree makes a nice **shade.**

(b) Shadow.

Don't say: The dog saw his shade in the water.
    Say: The dog saw his **shadow** in the water.

"Shade" is a place sheltered from the sun; "shadow" is a shade of a distinct form, as of a tree, a man, a dog, etc.

511. Customer and Client.

(a) Customer.

Don't say: That grocer has plenty of clients.
    Say: That grocer has plenty of **customers.**

(b) Client.

Don't say: That lawyer has plenty of customers.
    Say: That lawyer has plenty of **clients.**

A person can be a **customer** at a shop, but a **client** of a lawyer, a bank, etc.

CONFUSED WORDS

512. *Stranger* for **Guest.**

> *Don't say:* They had some strangers last night.
> *Say:* They had some **guests** last night.

A **"guest"** is usually a friend who comes to our house for a visit, while a **"stranger"** is a person unknown to us.

NOTE. A **"foreigner"** is a person born in another country and speaking a foreign language.

513. *Travel* for **Journey.**

> *Don't say:* Our travel to England was pleasant.
> *Say:* Our **journey** to England was pleasant.

"Journey" is the noun and **"travel"** is the verb, used to describe any method of moving from one place to another.

NOTE. We use the noun **"travel"** (1) in a general sense: as, "She loves **travel**"; (2) in the plural: as, "He has written a book about his **travels**."

514. *Foot* for **Leg.**

> *Don't say:* I hurt my foot—**if the injury is any-where above the ankle.**
> *Say:* I hurt my **leg.**

"Leg" is the part of the body from the hip down to the ankle, and **"foot"** is the part below the ankle. (**"Hand"** must also be carefully distinguished from **"arm."**)

NOTE. The **"leg"** of a chair, a table, a bed; the **"foot"** of a hill, a wall, a ladder, a page.

515. *Finger* for **Toe.**

> *Don't say:* I hurt a finger of my right foot.
> *Say:* I hurt a **toe** of my right foot.

"Fingers" are on the hand, and **"toes"** are on the foot.

516. *Poetry* for **Poem.**

> *Don't say:* I have a poetry to learn by heart.
> *Say:* I have a **poem** to learn by heart.

"Poetry" is the form of literature dealing with poems; a **"poem"** is one piece of poetry.

COMMON MISTAKES IN ENGLISH

517. *Theatre* for **Play.**

> *Don't say:* We shall have a theatre tonight.
> *Say:* We shall have a **play** tonight.

A "theatre" is a building in which plays are acted, not the "play" itself.

518. *Play* for **Game.**

> *Don't say:* They had a nice play of football.
> *Say:* They had a nice **game** of football.

Avoid using "play" in the sense of "game." "Play" means amusement: as, "He is fond of **play**."

519. *Dress* for **Suit.**

> *Don't say:* My elder brother has a new dress.
> *Say:* My elder brother has a new **suit.**

Girls and women wear "**dresses**"; boys and men wear "**suits.**" "**Clothes**" may denote either a dress or a suit: as, "John (*or* Mary) is wearing new **clothes.**"

NOTE. But we say "a man **in full dress, evening dress,** or **morning dress.**"

520. *Gentleman* for **Man.**

> *Don't say:* I have met a fat gentleman today.
> *Say:* I have met a fat **man** today.

It is best to use "**gentleman**" only when referring to a man's character: as, "He is a real **gentleman**"; or, "He is not a **gentleman.**"

521. *Individual* for **Person.**

> *Don't say:* Only five individuals were present.
> *Say:* Only five **persons** were present.

"**Individual**" is used of a single person as opposed to the group: as, "The **individual** must act for the good of the community."

CONFUSED WORDS

522. *Men* for **People.**

Don't say: All the streets were full of men.
Say: All the streets were full of **people.**

"People" and not "men" should be used when the reference is to human beings in general.

523. *Woman* for **Wife.**

Don't say: The man took his woman with him.
Say: The man took his **wife** with him.

In English, these two words are carefully distinguished: "woman" should not be used instead of "wife."

524. *Cost* for **Price.**

Don't say: What is the cost of this watch?
Say: What is the **price** of this watch?

"Price" is the amount of money paid by the customer; "cost" is the amount paid by the shopkeeper. But we can say "How much does it cost?"

NOTE. "Value" is the usefulness or importance of something: as, The **value** of milk as a food, the **value** of education. "Face value" is the amount printed on a piece of paper-money or on a postage stamp.

525. *Air* for **Wind.**

Don't say: The strong air blew his hat away.
Say: The strong **wind** blew his hat away.

"Air" is what we breathe, and "wind" is what makes the leaves of the trees move.

526. *Ground* for **Floor.**

Don't say: When I entered the room, I saw a book on the ground.
Say: When I entered the room, I saw a book on the **floor.**

The "floor" is the part of the room on which we walk; the "ground" is outside the house.

527. *Place* for **Room.**

> *Don't say:* Is there place for me in the bus?
> *Say:* Is there **room** for me in the bus?

"Place" cannot be used in the sense of **"room,"** which means here **"unoccupied space."**

528. *Organ* for **Instrument.**

> *Don't say:* What other organ can you play?
> *Say:* What other **instrument** can you play?

"Organ" cannot be used to denote any musical instrument; the **"organ"** is a particular musical **instrument** used in some churches to accompany the singing of hymns.

529. *Appetite* for **Desire,** etc.

> *Don't say:* I have no appetite at all to study.
> *Say:* I have no **desire** at all to study.

"Appetite" is generally used of food. For study, work, or play we use such words as **"desire," "disposition,"** and **"inclination."**

(See also Exercise 7 on page 151.)

(See also Exercise 7 on page 151.)

CONFUSION OF NUMBER

(*a*) The following cannot be used in the plural:

530. **Advice.**

> *Don't say:* He gave me some good advices.
> *Say:* He gave me some good **advice.**

NOTE. When only one thing is meant we say, **"a piece of advice"**: as, "Let me give you a **piece of advice.**"

531. **Information.**

> *Don't say:* Can you give me any informations?
> *Say:* Can you give me any **information**?

CONFUSED WORDS

NOTE. When only one thing is meant we say **"an item or a bit of information"**: as, "He gave me a useful **item of information."**

532. Furniture.

Don't say: Furnitures are often made of wood.
Say: **Furniture** is often made of wood.

NOTE. **"Furniture"** is a singular noun and always takes **a** singular verb and pronoun. **"A piece of furniture"** means **one** thing only.

533. Luggage.

Don't say: His luggages are at the station.
Say: His **luggage** is at the station.

NOTE. **"Baggage,"** another word for **"luggage,"** cannot be used in the plural either: as, "The **baggage** is ready for the train."

534. Damage.

Don't say: The fire caused many damages.
Say: The fire caused much **damage.**

NOTE. The plural form **"damages"** denotes money paid to make good a loss: as, "The insurance company paid the man **damages."**

535. Work.

Don't say: Today I have many works to do.
Say: Today I have a lot of **work** to do.

NOTE. The plural form **"works"** means a factory or the writings of an author: as, "The **works** of Shakespeare are many": "I visited the iron **works."**

536. Character.

Don't say: The school builds good characters.
Say: The school builds good **character.**

NOTE. The plural form **"characters"** denotes the letters of the alphabet or the persons in a book or play.

537. Hair.

Don't say: That woman has beautiful hairs.
Say: That woman has beautiful **hair.**

NOTE. But when **"hair"** is used to denote a single thread, the plural form is **"hairs"**: as, "I found two long **hairs** in my food."

538. Bread.

Don't say: Breads are sold at the baker's.
Say: **Bread** is sold at the baker's.

NOTE. But we can say **"a loaf of bread"** and **"loaves of bread"**: as, "I bought **a loaf** (two, three, etc., **loaves) of bread."**

539. Fish.

Don't say: Yesterday we had fishes for dinner.
Say: Yesterday we had **fish** for dinner.

NOTE. **"Fish"** as food or in bulk (= large numbers) is always singular. The plural form (**"fishes"**) is now rarely used and denotes fish individually: as, "I caught three small **fishes."**

540. Fruit.

Don't say: We haven't many fruits in summer.
Say: We haven't much **fruit** in summer.

NOTE. The plural form **"fruits"** is rarely used and means different kinds of fruit: as, "Cyprus produces oranges, apricots, and other **fruits."**

541. Grass.

Don't say: The dog lay down on the grasses.
Say: The dog lay down on the **grass.**

542. Dozen.

Don't say: I want to buy three dozens eggs.
Say: I want to buy three **dozen** eggs.

NOTE. But when **"dozen"** is not preceded by a numeral (like **"three"**) or by **"a"**, the plural form is used: as, "There were **dozens** of eggs."

CONFUSED WORDS

543. Hundred, etc.

Don't say: The town has fifty thousands people.
Say: The town has fifty **thousand** people.

NOTE. But **"hundred," "thousand,"** and **"million"** take the plural form if they are not preceded by a numeral or by **"a"** : as, **"Thousands** of people were present."

544. Sheep.

Don't say: Ten sheeps are grazing in the field.
Say: Ten **sheep** are grazing in the field.

NOTE. **"Sheep," "deer," "salmon,"** and a few other nouns have the same form for singular and plural. Thus, we say **"one sheep"** or **"ten sheep."**

545. Knowledge.

Don't say: He has good knowledges of history.
Say: He has a good **knowledge** of history.

546. Progress.

Don't say: The boy has made great progresses.
Say: The boy has made great **progress.**

547. Thunder and Lightning.

Don't say: There were thunders and lightnings.
Say: There was **thunder** and **lightning.**

NOTE. When only one thing is meant we say "a **crash** of thunder" and "a **flash** of lightning."

548. Machinery.

Don't say: They are now using new machineries.
Say: They are now using new **machinery.**

NOTE. **"Machinery"** is a singular noun and always takes a singular verb and pronoun. But we can say **"a piece of machinery"** or "pieces of machinery."

549. Mathematics, etc. + singular verb.

> *Don't say:* Mathematics are not easy to learn.
> *Say:* **Mathematics is** not easy to learn.

NOTE. The names of sciences and subjects ending in "-ics" (like "mathematics," "physics," "politics," "gymnastics") generally take a singular verb.

550. Money + singular verb.

> *Don't say:* All his money are kept in the bank.
> *Say:* All his **money is** kept in the bank.

NOTE. "Money" is a singular noun and always takes a singular verb and pronoun.

551. News + singular verb.

> *Don't say:* I am glad that the news are good.
> *Say:* I am glad that the **news is** good.

NOTE. "News," though plural in form, always takes a singular verb. If only one thing is meant we say **"a piece or an item of news"**: as, "This is a good **piece of news.**"

(*b*) The following cannot be used in the singular:

552. Scissors, etc. + plural verb.

> *Don't say:* The scissor is lying on the table.
> *Say:* The **scissors are** lying on the table.

NOTE. All names of things consisting of two parts (like "scissors," "trousers," "spectacles," "shears," "pliers") take a plural verb. But we can say "A pair of (scissors, etc.) is . . ."

553. People + plural verb.

> *Don't say:* There is much people in the cinema.
> *Say:* There **are** many **people** in the cinema.

NOTE. "People," meaning "nation," is singular; the plural is "peoples": as, "The Greeks are a brave people"; "The peoples of Europe are often engaged in war."

CONFUSED WORDS

554. Clothes + plural verb.

Don't say: Your cloth is an excellent fit.
Say: Your **clothes are** an excellent fit.

NOTE. "Cloth," meaning the material of which clothes are made, is singular, and has a plural form **"cloths"** (without the **"e"**): as, "She cleaned the table with a **cloth**"; "Merchants sell different kinds of **cloths**."

555. Riches + plural verb.

Don't say: It is said that riches has wings.
Say: It is said that **riches have** wings.

NOTE. "Riches" is a plural noun and always takes a plural verb.

556. Wages + plural verb.

Don't say: He complains that his wage is low.
Say: He complains that his **wages are** low.

NOTE. "Wages" is a plural noun and takes a plural verb. But we say "a living **wage**."

557. Billiards.

Don't say: Billiard is a very difficult game.
Say: **Billiards** is a very difficult game.

NOTE. "Billiards," "draughts," "darts" are always plural, but are followed by verbs in the singular.

558. Misuse of the adjective in the plural.

Don't say: It is our duty to help the poors.
Say: It is our duty to help the **poor.**

NOTE. Adjectives cannot take the plural form, even when they are used as nouns in the plural.

559. Misuse of "as well as" with a plural verb.

Don't say: Tom as well as George are coming.
Say: Tom **as well as** George **is** coming.

Two singular nouns joined by **"as well as"** require the verb to be singular.

560. Misuse of **"all"** (= everything) with a plural verb.

> *Don't say:* Nothing is left; all are lost.
> *Say:* Nothing is left; **all is** lost.

"All," meaning **everything**, takes a singular verb; **"all,"** meaning **everybody**, takes a plural verb, as, **"All** of us **are** present."

561. Misuse of the plural before **"kind"** or **"sort."**

> *Don't say:* I don't like these kind of games.
> *Say:* I don't like **this kind** of game.
> *Or:* I don't like games of **this kind.**

A demonstrative adjective must agree in number with the noun which it qualifies. In the sentence given, **"kind"** is singular and so should be the demonstrative adjective qualifying it.

562. Misuse of the plural with the name of a language.

> *Don't say:* English are easier than German.
> *Say:* **English is** easier than German.

Names of languages are singular and always take a singular verb.

563. Misuse of **"one"** and parts of **"one"** with the singular.

> *Don't say:* I read it in one and a half hour.
> *Say:* I read it in **one and a half hours.**

In English, the plural must be used with anything greater than one, even if it is less than two.

564. Misuse of the singular with a collective noun of plurality.

> *Don't say:* The class was divided in its opinion.
> *Say:* The class **were** divided in **their opinions.**

A collective noun usually takes a singular verb, but when it denotes the individual members of the group and not the group as a whole a plural verb must be used.

CONFUSED WORDS

565. "The number" and "A number."

(*a*) The number.

Don't say: The number of pupils are increasing.
    Say: **The number** of pupils **is** increasing.

(*b*) A number.

Don't say: A number of pupils is absent today.
    Say: **A number** of pupils **are** absent today.

When **"number"** is preceded by **"the"** it denotes a **unit** and is singular and is **"a"** it means **several** or **many** and is plural.

566. Misuse of "*This*" for "**These.**"

Don't say: This errors are made by foreigners.
    Say: **These** errors are made by foreigners.

"This" changes to **"these"** if the noun that follows is in the plural number.

NOTE. Avoid also the use of **"this"** instead of the personal pronoun. "John had the book but he gave this to his brother" should be "John had the book but he gave **it** to his brother."

567. Misuse of "*There is*" for "**There are.**"

Don't say: There is many boys waiting outside.
    Say: **There are** many **boys** waiting outside.

"There is" changes to **"there are"** if the noun that follows is in the plural number.

568. Misuse of "*You was*" for "**You were.**"

Don't say: You was very foolish to do that.
    Say: **You were** very foolish to do that.

"Was" is singular and **"were"** is plural, but with the pronoun **"you,"** even when it is singular in meaning, we always use **"were."**

NOTE. But in conditions and wishes, **"were"** may be used with the singular: as, "If I **were** you, I should go"; "I wish I **were** rich."

569. Misuse of "*life*," etc., for **"lives,"** etc.

Don't say: Many people lost their life at sea.
Say· Many people lost their **lives** at sea.

In English, words like **"life," "heart," "soul," "body," "mind"** are used in the plural when they refer to more than one person.

570. Non-agreement of the verb in number.

Don't say: A large supply of toys are expected.
Say: A large **supply** of toys **is** expected.

When the subject is singular, the verb must be singular; and when the subject is plural, the verb must be plural also. Care must be taken when a plural noun comes between a singular subject and its verb, as in the example above.

(See Exercises 1 and 2 on pages 149–150.)

CONFUSION OF PARTS OF SPEECH

571. As and **Like.**

(*a*) As.

Don't say: You do not play the game like I do.
Say: You do not play the game **as I do.**

(*b*) Like.

Don't say: You do not look as your brother.
Say: You do not look **like your brother.**

"As" is a conjunction, and is usually followed by a noun or pronoun in the nominative case. **"Like"** is not a conjunction, but an adjective which behaves like a preposition in being followed by a noun or pronoun in the objective case.

(See Exercise 93 on page 183.)

CONFUSED WORDS

Have another look at—
SINGULAR AND PLURAL

1. The plural of nouns is generally formed by adding -*s* or -*es* to the singular:

| book | church | knife | city | journey |
| books | churches | knives | cities | journeys |

2. The following nouns have irregular plurals:

Singular	*Plural*
man	men
woman	women
child	children
ox	oxen
tooth	teeth
foot	feet
goose	geese
mouse	mice

3. Some nouns are not used in the plural: as, *advice, information, knowledge, news, progress, work, money, luggage, furniture, scenery, machinery.*

NOTE. When only one thing is meant, we say *a piece of advice* (*information, news, work, money, furniture, luggage, machinery*).

4. Some nouns are not used in the singular: as, *people, riches, clothes, wages, trousers, scissors, spectacles.*

NOTE. Names of things consisting of two parts are often used with the word *pair*: as, *a pair of trousers* (*scissors, spectacles*, etc.).

5. Some nouns have the same form for the singular as for the plural: as, *sheep, deer, salmon.*

572. So and **Such.**

(*a*) So.

Don't say: It is such small that you cannot see it.
    Say: It is **so small** that you cannot see it.

(*b*) Such.

Don't say: I have never seen so large animal before.
    Say: I have never seen **such** a large **animal** before.

"So" is an adverb, and must qualify an adjective or another adverb; "such" is an adjective, and must qualify a noun.

573. No and **Not.**

(*a*) No.

Don't say: I have not mistakes in dictation.
    Say: I have **no mistakes** in dictation.

(*b*) Not.

Don't say: I have no any mistakes in dictation.
    Say: I have**n't** (= have **not**) **any** mistakes in dictation.

"No," meaning **not any**, is used as an adjective to qualify the noun. But if the noun is already qualified by an adjective, like **"any," "much," "enough,"** the adverb **"not"** must be used.

NOTE. "No" as an adverb is used only before a comparative: as, "I have **no more** to say."

(See Exercise 94 on page 183.)

574. Fool and **Foolish.**

(*a*) Fool.

Don't say: He said to me, "You are fool."
    Say: He said to me, "You are **a fool.**"

(*b*) Foolish.

Don't say: He said to me, "You are a foolish."
Say: He said to me, "You **are foolish**."

"Fool" is a noun, and requires the article when used with the verb "**to be**." "**Foolish**" is an adjective, and cannot be used with the article after the verb "**to be**."

NOTE. "**A fool**" or "**a foolish person**" does not mean an insane person, but one who acts thoughtlessly.

575. Misuse of **"due to"** as a preposition.

Don't say: He came late due to an accident.
Say: He came late **because of** an accident.

"Due to" should never be used as a preposition meaning **because of**. "Due," as an adjective here, is used correctly only when it qualifies some noun: as, "His delay was **due to** an accident."

576. Misuse of **"rest"** as an adjective.

Don't say: I spent the rest day at home.
Say: I spent **the rest of** the day at home.

Here, "**rest**" is a noun, and cannot be used as an adjective in the meaning of **what is left**.

577. Misuse of **"miser"** as an adjective.

Don't say: He loved money; he was miser.
Say: He loved money; he was **a miser**.

"Miser" is a noun, and cannot be used as an adjective. The adjective is "**miserly**": as, "He was **miserly**."

578. Misuse of **"opened"** as an adjective.

Don't say: I have found all the windows opened.
Say: I have found all the windows **open**.

The adjective is "**open**." The past participle is "**opened**": as, "Somebody has **opened** all the windows."

579. Misuse of **"friendly"** as an adverb.

Don't say: He behaves friendly.
Say: He behaves **in a friendly manner.**

The adverbial form is **"in a friendly manner."** **"Friendly"** is an adjective: as, a **friendly** game, to have **friendly** relations with one's neighbours, etc.

580. Misuse of **"truth"** as an adjective.

Don't say: Is it truth that he is very ill?
Say: **Is it true** that he is very ill?

"Truth" is not an adjective but a noun. The adjective is **"true,"** and is used with no article between it and the verb **"to be."**

581. Misuse of **"plenty"** as an adjective.

Don't say: He had plenty work to do.
Say: He had **plenty of work** to do.

"Plenty" is not an adjective, but a noun meaning a large number or amount. The adjective is **"plentiful"**: as, "Oranges are cheap now because they are **plentiful."**

582. Misuse of **"coward"** as an adjective.

Don't say: He said, "You are a coward boy."
Say: He said, "You are **a coward.**"

"Coward" (= one without courage) is the noun. The adjective is **"cowardly."**

583. Misuse of **"others"** as an adjective.

Don't say: The others boys are not present.
Say: The **other** boys are not present.

"Others" is not an adjective but a pronoun. The adjective is **"other"** (without the **"s"**). But we can say, "The **others** are not present," omitting the noun **"boys."**

584. Misuse of *"died"* for **"dead."**

Don't say: I think his grandfather is died.
Say: I think his grandfather is **dead.**

CONFUSED WORDS

"Died" is the past tense of "die." The adjective is "dead."

(See Exercise 95 on page 183.)

585. Misuse of "*shoot*" for "**shot.**"

> *Don't say:* I made a good shoot at the goal.
> *Say:* I made a good **shot** at the goal.

"Shoot" (in football) is the verb. The noun is "shot."

586. Misuse of "*it's*" for "**its.**"

> *Don't write:* The bird was feeding it's young.
> *Write:* The bird was feeding **its** young.

The possessive adjective "its" is correctly written without the apostrophe. So also "hers," "ours," "yours," "theirs" take no apostrophe.

(See Exercise 97 on page 184.)

587. Misuse of "*hot*" as a noun.

> *Don't say:* There is much hot this summer.
> *Say:* **It is very hot** this summer.

"Hot" is an adjective only, and cannot be used as a noun. The noun is "heat."

588. Misuse of "*pain*" as a verb.

> *Don't say:* I pain my leg *or* My leg is paining.
> *Say:* I **have** (*or* **feel**) **a pain** in my leg.

"Pain" is generally used as a noun, and is preceded by "have" or "feel."

589. Misuse of "*worth*" as a verb.

> *Don't say:* My bicycle worths seven pounds.
> *Say:* My bicycle **is worth** seven pounds.

"Worth" is not a verb, but an adjective.

COMMON MISTAKES IN ENGLISH

590. Misuse of "*able*" as a verb.

Don't say: The poor man does not able to pay.
Say: The poor man **is** not **able** to pay.

"**Able**" is an adjective, and cannot be used as a verb.

591. Misuse of "*afraid*" as a verb.

Don't say: John does not afraid of anybody.
Say: John **is** not **afraid** of anybody.

"**Afraid**" is not a verb but an adjective, and is generally used with the verb "**to be.**"

592. Misuse of "*weight*" as a verb.

Don't say: Have you weighted the letter?
Say: Have you **weighed** the letter?

"**Weight**" is a noun and cannot be used as a verb. The verb is "**weigh**" (without the "**t**").

593. Misuse of "*good*" for "**well.**"

Don't say: The goalkeeper plays very good.
Say: The goalkeeper **plays** very **well.**

"**Good**" is an adjective only, and cannot be used as an adverb.

(See Exercise 96 on page 184.)

594. Misuse of adjective for adverb.

Don't say: The little girl sang beautiful.
Say: The little girl **sang beautifully.**

An **adverb**, and not an adjective, should be used to qualify a verb.

NOTE. But after verbs such as "**look,**" "**feel,**" "**sound,**" "**taste,**" "**smell**" an adjective is used instead of an adverb: as, "Sugar tastes **sweet** (not sweetly)."

CONFUSED WORDS

595. Misuse of *"after"* for **"afterwards,"** etc.

> *Don't say:* After we went home for dinner.
> *Say:* **Afterwards** we went home for dinner.

"After" is a preposition and must be used with an object. "Afterwards," "then," "after that" are adverbs of time and can be used alone.

596. *"And the two,"* etc., used for **"both,"** etc.

> *Don't say:* I have seen and the two of them.
> *Say:* I have seen **both** of them.

Never say "and the two" instead of "both." Avoid also "and the three, four, etc." Say, "all three, four, etc."

597. Misuse of *"and"* for **"also"** or **"too."**

> *Don't say:* Let me do and the next exercise.
> *Say:* Let me do **also** the next exercise.
> *Or:* Let me do the next exercise **too.**

"And" is a conjunction, and can join only similar forms of speech: as, "He came **and** sat down." It cannot be used instead of the adverbs "also" and "too."

598. Misuse of *"and"* for **"even."**

> *Don't say:* He does not trust and his friends.
> *Say:* He does not trust **even** his friends.

"And" is a conjunction only, and cannot be used instead of the adverb "even."

599. Misuse of *"loose"* for **"lose."**

> *Don't say:* Be careful not to loose your money.
> *Say:* Be careful not to **lose** your money.

"Lose" (with one **o**) is the common verb meaning **not to be able to find.** "Loose" (with double **o**) is an adjective meaning **unfastened, free**: as, "The horse was **loose** in the field."

COMMON MISTAKES IN ENGLISH

600. Misuse of *"past"* for **"passed."**

Don't say: I past by your house yesterday.

Say: I **passed** by your house yesterday.

"Past" is not a verb. The past tense and past participle of the verb **"to pass"** is **"passed."**

NOTE. **"Past"** can be used as a noun, "Don't think of the **past**"; an adjective, "The **past** week was warm"; a preposition, "We walked **past** the church"; or an adverb, "The train went **past**."

(See Exercise 98 on page 184; see also Exercise 99 on page 185.)

EXERCISES

The following Exercises, which provide ample drill on the commonest mistakes dealt with in this book, are arranged under the headings of the various parts of speech.

TO THE STUDENT: Do not write *in the book* the answers to the Exercises.

NOUNS

CONFUSION OF NUMBER
(§§ 530–570)

EXERCISE 1.

Give the correct number, **is** or **are**, in the following:

1. The news I have received — good. 2. Where — the money? 3. His trousers — worn out. 4. Mathematics — my poorest subject. 5. Riches — sought after by all. 6. Our furniture — getting old. 7. This pair of scissors — not sharp. 8. Fish — not cheap today. 9. The number of newspapers — increasing. 10. The sheep — grazing in the field.

EXERCISE 2.

Correct the following sentences, giving reasons for your corrections:

1. His advices were very wise. 2. You was the first to

do it. 3. The class was not able to agree. 4. I have many works to do this morning. 5. The thunders and lightnings frightened the little girl. 6. I have more than two dozens of books at home. 7. The poors say that riches does not make a man happy. 8. He sent a man to bring his luggages. 9. You should go and have your hairs cut: they are too long. 10. I am waiting for more informations about this matter.

Exercise 3.

Write sentences showing whether the following nouns can be used in the singular or in the plural:

1. News. 2. Money. 3. Advice. 4. Riches. 5. Dozen. 6. Knowledge. 7. Spectacles. 8. Gymnastics. 9. Furniture. 10. Damage. 11. Hair. 12. Work.

NOUNS OFTEN CONFUSED
(§§ 503–529)

Exercise 4.

Use **house** or **home** in these sentences:

1. I live in a —. 2. My — is in Cyprus. 3. Many — are being built this year. 4. East or West, — is best. 5. The — was sold for £5,000. 6. Let us go inside the —.

Exercise 5.

Use **street** or **road** in these sentences:

1. The children were playing in the —. 2. This — leads to town. 3. This is the main — in the town. 4. The — of old towns are usually narrow. 5. They

are making a new — between the two towns. 6. What is the name of the — you live in?

Use **habit** or **custom** in these sentences:

1. Have you a — of washing your teeth? 2. It is the — of many people to pray for rain. 3. He has a — of biting his nails. 4. Smoking is not a good —. 5. The — of ants are very interesting. 6. The — of showing hospitality to strangers is very ancient.

Fill the blanks with one of the nouns in the brackets:

1. The ancient — of Greece is an interesting study (story, history). 2. His — swelled and he cannot get his shoe on (foot, leg). 3. The — spoilt the game (wind, air). 4. Mr. Brown is my lawyer and I have been his — for many years (customer, client). 5. We have a long — to learn by heart (poem, poetry). 6. He can play the violin and other — (organs, instruments). 7. The — of Switzerland is very beautiful (scene, scenery). 8. There was not much — anywhere (shade, shadow). 9. The ship was sunk in the — of the Atlantic (middle, centre). 10. The boys of the top class will do a — at the end of the year (theatre, play).

ADJECTIVES

COMPARATIVE OR SUPERLATIVE
(§§ 155–159, 483)

Rewrite the following with the adjectives between brackets in the correct degree:

COMMON MISTAKES IN ENGLISH

1. He is the (strong) boy in the whole school. 2. Of the two sisters Mary is the (beautiful). 3. Ann is the (young) of my four sisters. 4. John is the (old) of all my friends. 5. This is the (good) story I have ever read. 6. Which do you like (good), tea or coffee? 7. Iron is the (useful) of all metals. 8. The Nile is the (large) river in Africa. 9. Which of the two boys is (tall)? 10. George is (bad) than his brother.

EXERCISE 9.

Correct the following, giving reasons for your corrections:

1. Alexandria is smaller from Cairo. 2. New York is the larger city in the United States. 3. He is the better student from all. 4. John is more stronger than his brother. 5. I am two years elder than my sister. 6. Which is the heaviest, you or I? 7. Which of these three girls is the elder? 8. This boy's manners are more good than his brother's. 9. Which of the boys is the taller from the class? 10. Mount Everest is the higher mountain of the world.

ADJECTIVES OFTEN CONFUSED
(§§ 478–502)

EXERCISE 10.

Use **many** or **much** in these sentences:

1. He hasn't — money. 2. Have they — books? 3. There isn't — food in the house. 4. Does he take — interest in it? 5. I haven't — time. 6. Are there — pupils absent today? 7. How — does this book cost? 8. — rain has fallen on the mountains. 9. He doesn't

EXERCISES

know — English. 10. — drops of water go to make up the stream.

EXERCISE 11.

Use **few** or **a few**, **little** or **a little** in these sentences:

1. As he has — books, he is not able to study. 2. Will you have — wine? 3. He is very ill; there is — hope for him. 4. There are — apples in the basket, help yourself to some. 5. — people study Latin nowadays. 6. He cannot afford it as he has — money left. 7. As he did not speak clearly, — people understood what he said. 8. — people will admit their faults. 9. We must save — money for our journey home. 10. I have — friends in London who will help me.

EXERCISE 12.

Use **ill** or **sick** in these sentences:

1. She was suddenly taken —. 2. The meat was bad, and made everybody —. 3. He went to the hospital to visit the —. 4. The — man died yesterday. 5. When we are — we send for the doctor. 6. Those who are in bad health are said to be —. 7. The — and the wounded are taken to hospital. 8. He is — with a bad cold. 9. When I travel by boat I always become —. 10. He felt — and left in the middle of the game.

EXERCISE 13.

Use **some** or **any** in these sentences:

1. I have — new books at home. 2. There are not — flowers in the garden. 3. Have you — brothers in

school? 4. Did you buy — stamps from him? 5. Have I — letters this morning? 6. This magazine has — beautiful pictures.

Exercise 14.

Use **his** or **her** in these sentences:

1. The father called — daughter to come. 2. She gave the money to a neighbour of — uncle. 3. He sent a letter to — niece. 4. A woman lost — son. 5. The grandfather promised a nice gift to the eldest son of — daughter. 6. Mary sent a letter to — brother.

Exercise 15.

Use **interesting** or **interested** in these sentences:

1. I am — in English. 2. Was the film — last night? 3. The book is — from beginning to end. 4. She is a most — lady. 5. Are you — in sports? 6. Stamps are — only to those who are — in them.

Exercise 16.

Fill the blanks with one of the adjectives in the brackets:

1. He sat down and said nothing — (farther, further). 2. Is that the — edition of *The Times* (last, latest)? 3. Wash your hands if they are not — (clean, clear). 4. A prize was given to — one of the two best pupils (each, every). 5. He knows — words than his brother (less, fewer). 6. Several people were — when

EXERCISES

the train ran off the lines (wounded, injured). 7. John is — than his cousin (higher, taller). 8. Tom is five years old; he is too — to go to school (small, young). 9. George is my — brother (older, elder). 10. My brother George is — than I am (older, elder).

THE ARTICLES
(§§ 251–259, 308–328)

EXERCISE 17.

Fill the blanks with **a** or **an** where necessary.

1. Swimming is — great fun. 2. The aeroplane makes — noise. 3. What sort of — man is he? 4. My uncle made — fortune in America. 5. He has more than — thousand pounds. 6. The train left half — hour ago. 7. She has made — great progress in English. 8. She is — clever girl. 9. He tried without success to find — work. 10. Sunshine is necessary for — good health.

EXERCISE 18.

Fill the blanks with **the** where necessary:

1. My little brother will go to — school next year. 2. My father left — school many years ago. 3. I go to — cinema twice a week. 4. — cotton of Egypt is exported to many countries. 5. — Nile flows into — Mediterranean. 6. At what time is — lunch? 7. He can speak — French. 8. She speaks — German better than — English. 9. — flies are harmful insects. 10. The boy was sent to — prison to take a letter. 11. — football is a more popular game than — hockey. 12. — red, — blue, and — green are beautiful colours. 13. —

honesty is the best policy. 14. — British are not in the habit of paying compliments. 15. God made — country, and — man made — town.

PRONOUNS

EXERCISE 19.

Put relative pronouns in each of the following:

1. That is the boy — came yesterday. 2. The man to — I spoke is my brother. 3. The girl — mother is ill has left school. 4. This is the pen — I bought. 5. I cannot repeat all — I heard. 6. He is a boy — I know you can trust. 7. She is the girl — we thought had been ill. 8. He is the tallest man — I ever saw. 9. She is the same — she has always been. 10. I like to help those — I love and — I know love me.

EXERCISE 20.

Put interrogative pronouns in each of the following:

1. — do you find easier to learn, English or French? 2. About — were you talking? (The cinema.) 3. — is this book? (My uncle's.) 4. — of the two players do you like better? 5. — do you think I wanted? (Your brother.) 6. — of the three boys spoke? 7. — did you say won the prize? 8. — is he, do you suppose? (A

EXERCISES

lawyer.) 9. — of your brothers works in the bank?
10. — is the number of your house?

REPETITION OF SUBJECT OR OBJECT
(§§ 340–346)
EXERCISE 21.

Rewrite the following sentences, crossing out every unnecessary pronoun:

1. The prizes they were given to the boys. 2. The girl she said nothing. 3. The teacher gave us an exercise to do it. 4. He went home and he brought his book. 5. The book which it is on the table is mine. 6. Students who are good at their lessons they get good marks.. 7. He gave us a football to play with it. 8. The people having seen the game they went away. 9. The headmaster I have seen him just now. 10. The scorpion it has a sting in its tail.

MISCELLANEOUS EXAMPLES
EXERCISE 22.

Correct the following sentences, giving reasons for your corrections:

1. One should mind his own business. 2. The most of the people are fond of the cinema. 3. This is the boy which is always late. 4. I speak English better than him. 5. She told her mother all what had been said. 6. This cake is for you and myself. 7. I want to give me your book, please. 8. Is a very good girl. 9. It is them. 10. I and John are friends.

COMMON MISTAKES IN ENGLISH

VERBS

SEQUENCE OF TENSES
(§§ 108–111)

EXERCISE 23.

Put the verbs in brackets into the tenses required:

1. I thought that he (can) run much faster. 2. The boy said that he (begin) his work tomorrow. 3. He says he (understand) French very well. 4. The teacher said, "London (be) the largest city in the world." 5. The teacher said that London (be) the capital of England. 6. I was sure that he (shall) succeed. 7. I asked him if he (want) anything. 8. They say that he (shall) pass the examination. 9. She told me that she (feel) very tired. 10. The boy worked hard so that he (may) not fail in the examination.

EXERCISE 24.

Complete the following, using a verb in the required tense:

1. George told me that he —.
2. I asked him whether he —.
3. James said that he —.
4. Our teacher taught us that —.
5. He gave me a promise that he —.
6. The boys said that —.
7. I knew that he —.
8. I asked him to wait until —.
9. I thought that he —.
10. He did not come when —.

EXERCISES

EXERCISE 25.

Supply the correct tense, **Simple Present** or **Present Continuous,** in the following:

1. I (to go) to school every day. 2. He (to go) to the school now. 3. Look! They (to come) towards us. 4. Now I (to hear) him clearly. 5. Every morning I (to take) a walk by the riverside. 6. The sun (to rise) in the east and (to set) in the west. 7. The teacher (to watch) me when I (to write). 8. We (to go) to the cinema this evening. 9. I (to read) English now. 10. People (to use) umbrellas when it (to rain).

EXERCISE 26.

Supply the correct tense, **Past Tense** or **Past Continuous,** in the following:

1. When I (come) in, it (rain). 2. Many years ago people (travel) on horseback. 3. I (meet) him as I (go) home. 4. He (go) to another school last year. 5. My father (play) football in his youth. 6. We (eat) our dinner when he (come) to visit us. 7. In the past he (smoke) a great deal. 8. They (shout) when the teacher (enter) the room. 9. Last year he (study) very hard. 10. While he (play) football he (lose) his ring.

EXERCISE 27.

Supply the correct tense, **Past Tense** or **Present Perfect,** in the following:

COMMON MISTAKES IN ENGLISH

1. He (come) back last week. 2. I just (finish) my work. 3. I (live) in London last year. 4. The bell (ring) five minutes ago. 5. I (see) the Pyramids of Egypt. 6. This book first (print) in 1936. 7. He (be) ill of fever since last Saturday. 8. The ship (arrive) yesterday. 9. I (stay) at my uncle's last night. 10. I (deposit) the money in the bank.

Exercise 28.

Supply the correct tense, **Past Tense** or **Past Perfect,** in the following:

1. I (want) to see you yesterday. 2. He (tell) me that he (see) me the day before yesterday. 3. There (be) a strong wind last night. 4. The boy (find) the book which he (lose). 5. When I (run) a mile, I (be) very tired. 6. The tourist (speak) about the countries he (visit). 7. When I (be) a boy I (study) music. 8. The Romans (speak) Latin. 9. After he (finish) his work he (go) to bed. 10. He (sleep) an hour when I (awake) him.

Exercise 29.

Complete the following, using the correct tense:

1. We shall go for a picnic, if —.
2. I shall visit the Pyramids when —.
3. Some people talk as if —.
4. Since he came here —.
5. I should enjoy myself, if —.
6. You would have passed, if —.

160

EXERCISES

Exercise 30.

Rewrite the following with the verbs between brackets in the correct tense:

1. After he (finish) his work he (go) home. 2. I (study) English for two years. 3. I (finish) my work this morning. 4. I (write) my exercise before Tom (call) for me. 5. He said he (shall) go to the cinema. 6. I not (see) him since Wednesday. 7. I (speak) to him five minutes ago. 8. I (study) grammar last year. 9. She always (whisper) during the lesson. 10. The messenger (come) back.

Exercise 31.

Correct the following sentences, giving reasons for your corrections:

1. He said that he is working hard. 2. How long did you waited for me yesterday? 3. He speaks English very well, but I am not sure whether he can speaks French too. 4. He is on the team for two years. 5. I have seen him yesterday at church. 6. What do you do now?—I do my exercise. 7. I use to get up early. 8. He acts as if he is a rich man. 9. I shall speak to him as soon as he will come. 10. I told him to come with us, but he says that he is not feeling well.

THIRD PERSON SINGULAR
(§§ 246, 247).

Exercise 32.

Put the following into the third person singular, present tense:

1. I do my work carefully. 2. The fishermen catch

fish. 3. You have a new bicycle. 4. The teacher taught us English. 5. She walked to the station to catch the train. 6. They combed and brushed their hair. 7. He fell down and hurt his leg. 8. I say good morning to my parents and I begin my breakfast. 9. I sit and talk to my friends. 10. I go to school on my bicycle.

EXERCISE 33.

Fill the blanks with the right word, **don't** or **doesn't**, in the following:

1. I — think so. 2. John — know how to swim. 3. He — play football well. 4. It — matter what they say. 5. Some pupils — take good care of their books. 6. — you know where I live? 7. Why — you try? 8. Teachers — like lazy pupils. 9. He — speak English very well. 10. — be afraid of the dog.

QUESTIONS AND NEGATIONS
(§§ 105–106, 261, 371–372)

EXERCISE 34.

Rewrite the following sentences (a) as questions, (b) as negative sentences:

1. He went home. 2. You told me to wait. 3. I made a mistake. 4. He broke the window. 5. She did the exercise. 6. He speaks English. 7. He bought a new hat. 8. She found her book. 9. Mary came late. 10. He knew the answer.

EXERCISE 35.

Answer the following questions (a) in the affirmative, (b) in the negative, using complete sentences:

EXERCISES

1. Did you buy a new bicycle? 2. Does John swim across the river? 3. Did you find the book that you lost? 4. Does he ring the bell? 5. Did he go to London last year? 6. Did he teach you anything? 7. Did you know the answer to the problem? 8. Does he speak many languages? 9. Did you think it would rain? 10. Did they catch the thief?

EXERCISE 36.

Correct whatever is wrong with the following questions:

1. You were at the cinema last night? 2. At what time did he came yesterday? 3. You will go home next week? 4. He has returned from leave? 5. Does she speaks French? 6. You have some good news for me? 7. He can drive a car? 8. You heard about the accident? 9. Why he comes here every day? 10. When the post will come?

QUESTION PHRASES (§ 167)

EXERCISE 37.

Complete the following, adding question phrases:
1. She sings well, — ?
2. He can't swim, — ?
3. You play the piano, — ?
4. He struck the boy, — ?
5. It is cool today, — ?
6. It isn't warm today, — ?

COMMON MISTAKES IN ENGLISH

INDIRECT QUESTIONS (§ 375)

Exercise 38.

Change the following into indirect questions:

1. I said to him, "What is your idea?" 2. We said to them, "Where are you going?" 3. I said to him, "How much did you pay for your bicycle?" 4. I said to the man, "What is the price of this book?" 5. He said to the guest, "Do you want tea or coffee?" 6. He said to me, "Did you ring the bell?" 7. The tourist said to us, "Where is the road to the station?" 8. The teacher said to me, "Why are you weeping?" 9. He said to me, "Why are you late?" 10. He said, "How long does it take you to reach home?"

DOUBLE NEGATIVE (§ 170)

Exercise 39.

Rewrite the following sentences correctly, in two ways:

1. I could not find him nowhere. 2. There isn't no one here who knows his name. 3. I didn't see nobody there. 4. He did not tell me nothing. 5. He is not neither wise nor good. 6. You will not find the box nowhere. 7. We did not give him nothing. 8. I don't know nothing. 9. He did not speak to no one in the room. 10. Nobody never saw him without his stick.

CONTRACTIONS (§ 387)

Exercise 40.

Write the words for which each of the following contractions stands:

EXERCISES

1. Don't. 2. Doesn't. 3. Aren't. 4. Isn't. 5. Wasn't. 6. Can't. 7. Couldn't. 8. Haven't. 9. We'll. 10. You've.

EXERCISE 41.

Write contractions for the following:

1. Would not. 2. I am. 3. I have. 4. I will. 5. Had not. 6. He is. 7. It is. 8. Will not. 9. Shall not. 10. Must not.

VERBS OFTEN CONFUSED
(§§ 406–466)

EXERCISE 42.

Supply **shall** or **will** in the following:

1. Tomorrow — be Sunday. 2. All right, I — come. 3. You — not leave this room until you finish your work. 4. You — find your books on the table. 5. — I bring my books with me? 6. He — go to school this year. 7. No! I — never do that. 8. I — write a few letters tomorrow. 9. I — do it whether they like it or not. 10. "We — be as quiet as mice," promised the children.

EXERCISE 43.

Supply some form of **say** or **tell** in the following:

1. He always — the truth. 2. John —, "I shall go tomorrow." 3. She — nothing. 4. They — that he is ill. 5. He — that he would go the next day. 6. I — him that I should go with him. 7. He — to me, "I am not feeling well." 8. What is he —ing? 9. Don't — lies. 10. He — me that he would go home.

COMMON MISTAKES IN ENGLISH

EXERCISE 44.

Supply some form of **make** or **do** in the following:

1. The best cloth is — in England. 2. He — his best to help me. 3. Have you — your homework? 4. I have only — my duty. 5. If you take this medicine, it will — you good. 6. — whatever you like. 7. What were you —ing when I came in? 8. Do you — your exercises carefully? 9. Don't — a noise. 10. I have a difficult problem to —.

EXERCISE 45.

Supply some form of **lie** or **lay** in the following:

1. I shall go and — down. 2. The book was —ing on the floor. 3. He — down to rest. 4. — down, Fox. 5. The hen has — an egg. 6. How long have you — in bed? 7. He — to the teacher. 8. He ordered his men to — down. 9. I — the book on the table. 10. Yesterday she — in bed until midday.

EXERCISE 46.

Supply some form of **sit, seat,** or **set** in the following:

1. Please — down. 2. Please — yourself. 3. Please be —. 4. The sun — in the west. 5. The boat will — twelve people. 6. The old man was —ing by the fire. 7. — the vase on the table. 8. The dog was —ing on the chair. 9. The teacher — the boys as they came in. 10. I once — in that famous chair.

EXERCISES

EXERCISE 47.

Supply some form of **rise** or **raise** in the following:

1. Prices — during the war. 2. He promised to — the man's wages. 3. The balloon — in the sky. 4. The sun — at six o'clock. 5. He — his hat to the teacher. 6. The box is too heavy; I can't — it. 7. He — from his seat and left the room. 8. I — very early in the morning. 9. The teacher told him to — his voice. 10. We had — from table before he came in.

EXERCISE 48.

Supply some form of **wear, put on,** or **dress** in the following:

1. She always — a green hat. 2. I — my hat and went out. 3. The mother — the child. 4. She — a beautiful dress at the dance. 5. It takes him much time to — his clothes. 6. He — a red tie yesterday. 7. She never — brown shoes. 8. Mary — herself and went to the party. 9. I shall — my new dress at the wedding. 10. When he came in he was —ing his hat.

EXERCISE 49.

Supply some form of **let, let go, leave,** or **give up** in the following:

1. — your books here. 2. Does your father — you go swimming? 3. Please — my room. 4. I have — music. 5. Where have you — your pen? 6. Mother will not — me go. 7. His old friends — him. 8. Please — my hand. 9. Someone always — the door open. 10. — me go, too.

COMMON MISTAKES IN ENGLISH

EXERCISE 50.

Supply some form of **fly, flow,** or **flee** in the following:

1. The aeroplane — over the city. 2. The birds have — north for the summer. 3. He — from danger. 4. The water — all day. 5. The flies — through the window. 6. The Nile — into the Mediterranean. 7. He — from London to New York. 8. The prisoner has — from his guard. 9. Birds —. 10. The wild horses — from the men.

EXERCISE 51.

Supply **hung** or **hanged** in the following:

1. He was found guilty and —. 2. Mother — the clothes up to dry. 3. The picture — on the wall. 4. The criminal was —. 5. He — his hat up.

EXERCISE 52.

Supply some form of **borrow** or **lend** in the following:

1. May I — your pen? 2. Please — me your book. 3. From whom did you — the money? 4. He will — you his knife. 5. You should avoid —ing things from others.

EXERCISE 53.

Supply some form of **steal** or **rob** in the following:

1. They — the house and fled. 2. Someone has — his money. 3. "I have been —," cried the lady. 4. When the bank was —, the robbers escaped. 5. The cat will — the dog's meat.

EXERCISES

EXERCISE 54.

Supply some form of **refuse** or **deny** in the following:

1. He — to do the work. 2. John — that he had seen him. 3. Do you — that you broke the window? 4. I — to take the money. 5. I asked him to come with us, but he —.

EXERCISE 55.

Supply **can** or **may** in the following:

1. — you play the piano? 2. I am sure that you — do better. 3. — I leave the book with you? 4. — I speak to you for a moment? 5. You — go now, if you like.

EXERCISE 56.

Supply some form of **learn** or **teach** in the following:

1. She — her friends the new game. 2. Will you — me how to swim? 3. He — his lessons quickly. 4. My teacher — me English. 5. The pupils — their lessons.

EXERCISE 57.

Supply some form of **win** or **beat** in the following:

1. We were sure to —. 2. I can — him at chess. 3. The shield was — by our school. 4. We have — your team several times. 5. We have always —.

EXERCISE 58.

Supply some form of **see** or **look** in the following:

1. We cannot — in the dark. 2. Don't — out of the

window. 3. Do you — that man? 4. It is not proper to — through an open window. 5. The blind cannot —.

EXERCISE 59.

Supply some form of **hear** or **listen** in the following:

1. I — carefully but — nothing. 2. He cannot — very well. 3. I was —ing to the music. 4. The deaf cannot —. 5. Let us — to the story.

EXERCISE 60.

Supply some form of **like** or **want** in the following:

1. I — to go to Athens next year. 2. Children — to play. 3. Do you — to come with me for a drive? 4. He always — to get up early. 5. Do you — to play tennis this afternoon?

EXERCISE 61.

Supply some form of **read** or **study** in the following:

1. My father — *The Times*. 2. The boy is —ing his lessons. 3. When I finish —ing geography, I shall — the letter. 4. She — a lot, but she doesn't — her lessons. 5. When the boys have — their lessons, they are allowed to — magazines.

EXERCISE 62.

Supply **fall** or **fell** in the following:

1. Did the child — from the chair? 2. The aeroplane — into the sea. 3. He — down and broke his leg. 4. In winter the leaves — from the trees. 5. You will — if you are not careful.

EXERCISES

EXERCISE 63.

In the following sentences, choose the correct word from those in the brackets:

1. Who (discovered, invented) the telephone? 2. The judge was (persuaded, convinced) that the man was guilty. 3. When will the meeting (take place, take part)? 4. He (took, received) a prize for his diligence. 5. It is not wise to (interfere with, interfere in) family quarrels. 6. He (is, is found) at the school in the morning. 7. At what time do˙you (sleep, go to bed)? 8. She did not (accept, agree) to go. 9. A butcher (deals in, deals with) meat. 10. How does that man (win, earn) his living? 11. If you take 3 from 7, 4 (remain, stay). 12. Please (remember, remind) me to give the money back. 13. The judge (revenged, avenged) the wrong done to the child. 14. I (pleased, asked) him to post a letter for me. 15. Some people (like, love) freedom so much that they are ready to die for it.

UN-ENGLISH EXPRESSIONS
(§§ 189–226)

EXERCISE 64.

Correct the following sentences, giving the true idiom:

1. Few people will admit that they have wrong. 2. Every day I put my watch with the church bell. 3. Will there be a game today afternoon? 4. He brought˙a good example. 5. Slowly, slowly, don't make a noise. 6. The teacher did not put us a new lesson. 7. Come down from the bicycle. 8. When do you make your bath? 9. I have much work; I need an hour to do it. 10. Many Englishmen drink a pipe.

171

11. I close the lights before I sleep. 12. How are you going with your music lessons? 13. I cut my hair twice a month. 14. Every morning I go for a walk with my bicycle. 15. The boy could not give the examination because he was ill. 16. Did you follow the game yesterday? 17. What film will be played on Sunday? 18. What have you and you are sad? 19. I make exercise every morning. 20. The teacher put me a good mark because I knew the poem from out.

MISUSE OF THE INFINITIVE
(§§ 76–104)
EXERCISE 65.

Put a suitable gerund in the place of each of these dashes:

1. Do this without — any mistakes. 2. We do not enjoy —. 3. He succeeded in — the door. 4. I cannot prevent you from —. 5. It's no use — about everything. 6. He stopped — in class. 7. I was busy — ready for dinner. 8. It's worth — well. 9. I think of — to London next year. 10. It's no use — over spilt milk.

EXERCISE 66.

Make sentences of your own, using a gerund after each of the following:

1. Avoid. 2. Instead of. 3. Stop. 4. Finish. 5. Tired. 6. Prevent. 7. Interested. 8. Worth. 9. Insist. 10. Can't help. 11. Fond. 12. Think.

EXERCISES

EXERCISE 67.

Make sentences of your own, using an infinitive after each of the following verbs:

1. Can. 2. Could. 3. May. 4. Might. 5. Must. 6. Let. 7. Make. 8. See. 9. Hear. 10. Feel.

ADVERBS

WRONG POSITION OF ADVERBS
(§§ 362–369)

EXERCISE 68.

Rewrite the following sentences, placing the adverbs or adverbial phrases in the right position:

1. I can speak very well English. 2. I like very much music. 3. A beginner cannot speak correctly English. 4. The teacher explained very well the problem. 5. The hunter shot with his gun a lion. 6. He put into his pocket the money. 7. He likes very much wine. 8. He learnt by heart the poem. 9. I received from my uncle a nice present. 10. He shut quickly the book.

EXERCISE 69.

Rewrite the following sentences, placing **only** in the right position:

1. We have only lost one game. 2. He only was married yesterday. 3. I am only left. 4. These people only seem to live for pleasure. 5. We only had one orange between us. 6. She only wrote on one side of

the paper. 7. The office is only open in the morning. 8. John was only punished; the others were not. 9. I only have five pence left. 10. I only spoke to him once after that.

EXERCISE 70.

Correct the following sentences, giving reasons for your corrections:

1. I always am on time. 2. It rains seldom in the desert. 3. We went yesterday there. 4. I am not enough tall. 5. He begged the teacher to not punish him. 6. I could have not arrived sooner. 7. He will have not finished his work by tomorrow. 8. I prefer usually coffee to tea. 9. They are leaving for London this evening at seven o'clock. 10. John yesterday did not come to school.

ADVERBS OFTEN CONFUSED
(§§ 467–477)

EXERCISE 71.

Give the correct adverb, **very** or **too**, in these sentences:

1. It is — cold today. 2. He is — old to work. 3. I can't drink the milk: it's — sweet. 4. Sugar is — sweet. 5. This hat is — small for me. 6. Eiffel Tower is — high. 7. The aeroplane flies — fast. 8. My little brother is — young to go to school. 9. I felt — tired to study. 10. He is — rich: he is a millionaire.

EXERCISES
EXERCISE 72.

Give the correct adverb, **very** or **much**, in these sentences:

1. I am — sorry that you cannot come. 2. I was — pleased to meet him. 3. She was — afraid of failing in English. 4. It was a — amusing game. 5. I feel — tired. 6. He plays — better than his brother. 7. His composition is — worse than yours. 8. It is a — interesting book. 9. I was — interested to hear what he said. 10. We are — astonished at the news.

EXERCISE 73.

Give the correct adverb, **very much** or **too much**, in these sentences:

1. I like oranges —. 2. Thank you —. 3. I can't study here: there is — noise. 4. Fifty pence is — for that book. 5. He drank — and became sick. 6. I was — astonished to hear of his coming. 7. She speaks —: she is a chatterbox. 8. I am — obliged to you. 9. She was — interested in the subject. 10. He helped us —.

EXERCISE 74.

Give the correct adverb, **hard** or **hardly**, in these sentences:

1. The man was hit very —. 2. I — know how to thank you for your kindness. 3. He has — recovered from his illness. 4. If you work —, perhaps you can succeed. 5. Think — before you come to a decision. 6. He tried — but failed.

COMMON MISTAKES IN ENGLISH

Exercise 75.

Make six sentences of your own, using the word **ago**.

PREPOSITIONS

USING A WRONG PREPOSITION
(§§ 1–75)

Exercise 76.

Fill the blanks with suitable prepositions:

1. I was not pleased — him. 2. Cats are afraid — dogs. 3. Look — this new book. 4. We are proud — our country. 5. He feels ashamed — his low marks. 6. We arrived — the station late. 7. She is very different — her sister. 8. Are you satisfied — your bicycle? 9. I am not accustomed — life in a hotel. 10. Many people complain — their low wages. 11. The judge suspected the witness — lying. 12. My brother is interested — stamps. 13. The policeman took the lady — the arm. 14. We should not spend our money — useless things. 15. A wise man is careful — his money. 16. Divide the apple — three parts. 17. Examination papers are usually written — ink. 18. He is angry — you. 19. I prefer honesty — deceit. 20. Travelling — ship or — train is far more comfortable than travelling — horseback or — a bicycle. 21. I am not indifferent — your happiness. 22. They exchange cloth — rubber. 23. I shall be dependent — my parents until I can earn my living. 24. This diary is not similar — the one I bought last year. 25. I would not advise you to have confidence — him.

EXERCISES

EXERCISE 77.

Rewrite the following sentences, using the correct prepositions:

1. He was accused for lying. 2. I am surprised from the news. 3. I am interested for fishing. 4. We believe to God. 5. Water is composed from oxygen and hydrogen. 6. Are you sure for his honesty? 7. The cat was guilty for stealing meat. 8. He was finally cured from the habit of drinking. 9. He is very good in English. 10. When is he leaving to England? 11. Many birds live with seeds. 12. I cannot get rid from this cold. 13. This cloth is superior from that. 14. Some people are jealous from their friends. 15. We must get rid from these insects. 16. He grew tired from walking and sat down to rest. 17. Can you translate this letter to English? 18. That depends entirely from you. 19. She was dressed with a yellow dress. 20. Pupils who are weak at lessons are often good in games. 21. He did his best to comply to the regulations. 22. If you persist on doing that, I shall be angry against you. 23. This is much inferior from the one I bought last week. 24. His composition was full with mistakes. 25. Everything in the room was covered by dust.

EXERCISE 78.

Write sentences, using the following words with suitable prepositions:

aim	boast	insist	marry
deprive	die	different	fail
repent	succeed	good	interested

| afraid | used | look | satisfied |
| pleased | ashamed | depend | prefer |

EXERCISE 79.

Make sentences of your own, showing clearly the difference between the following:

1. Arrive at; arrive in. 2. Angry with; angry at. 3. Pleased with; pleased at. 4. Look at; look for. 5. Write with; write in. 6. Divide in; divide into. 7. Die of; die from. 8. Disappointed in; disappointed of. 9. Sit at; sit on. 10. Tired of; tired with.

PREPOSITIONS OFTEN CONFUSED
(§§ 389–405)

EXERCISE 80.

Use **to** or **at** in these sentences:

1. He goes — market every morning. 2. He stood — the window. 3. The boy is — school. 4. I met him — the station. 5. I am going — a party tonight. 6. I enjoyed myself — the party. 7. The tourist stayed — the Palace Hotel. 8. After his illness, he returned — his work. 9. I saw him — the cinema. 10. Please wait for me — the gate.

EXERCISE 81.

Use **in** or **at** in these sentences:

1. There are high buildings — New York. 2. I live — a small village. 3. I spent my childhood — Greece. 4. My friend was born — Ceylon. 5. He studied — Oxford. 6. She lives — Luxor — Egypt. 7. It is more

expensive living — London than — Brighton. 8. He
lives — Paris. 9. Diamonds are found — Kimberley —
South Africa. 10. He lives here — —.

EXERCISE 82.

Use **in** or **into** in these sentences:

1. The fish swim — the river. 2. The man jumped —
the river. 3. They were standing — the room. 4. We
are — the classroom now. 5. There is a bird — the
cage. 6. We walked — the next room. 7. The children are playing — the field. 8. He poured the water —
the jug. 9. She dived — the water. 10. The river
flows — the sea.

EXERCISE 83.

Use **at, in,** or **on** in these sentences:

1. He was born — 1944. 2. — winter the weather is
cold. 3. — Christmas Day I received many gifts. 4.
We reached Cairo — nine o'clock. 5. The train arrived
— night. 6. There is a holiday — the 11th of December. 7. People return from their work — noon. 8. —
July the weather is warm. 9. — the afternoon I go for
a walk. 10. The train will arrive — Tuesday — eleven
o'clock — the morning.

EXERCISE 84.

Use **beside** or **besides** in these sentences:

1. There is a road — the river. 2. He sat — me.
3. There was no one there — John and me. 4. Come
and sit — me. 5. Have you any other books — these?

6. The mother sat — the sick child. 7. — my mother tongue I can speak English and French. 8. The cat lay — the fire. 9. Mrs. Smith is walking — Mr. Smith. 10. There are many others, — me.

EXERCISE 85.

Use **between** or **among** in these sentences:

1. The work was shared — all. 2. He divided the money — his three children. 3. He hid — the trees. 4. The officer walked — the two lines of soldiers. 5. — all those boys, he had not a single friend. 6. There was a fight — the two friends. 7. The ball passed — the goal-posts. 8. We are — friends. 9. His subject was "Life — the Eskimos." 10. The cake was divided — the two boys.

EXERCISE 86.

In the following sentences, choose the correct preposition from those in the brackets:

1. He has been ill (from, since) last Friday. 2. You have sold your bicycle (at, for) a good price. 3. I sold my bicycle (at, for) six pounds. 4. I expect to return (after, in) a week. 5. I can wait (to, till) next Tuesday. 6. We draw lines (by, with) a ruler. 7. He has been absent (since, for) a month. 8. They spoke (for, about) the weather. 9. He worked (with, by) the light of a candle. 10. You can send the parcel (with, by) post.

EXERCISE 87.

Write sentences of your own to show clearly the difference between the following pairs of prepositions:

EXERCISES

1. Beside; besides. 2. Between; among. 3. To; till. 4. In; into. 5. To; at. 6. For; at (price). 7. With; by. 8. For; since. 9. For; about. 10. In; within.

OMISSION OF PREPOSITIONS
(§§ 227–245)

EXERCISE 88.

Supply the prepositions omitted in the following:

1. Somebody is knocking the door. 2. I am searching my lost book. 3. He said me, "I shall not come." 4. He explained him the difficult words. 5. She never listens her mother. 6. I replied his letter at once. 7. Do you wish anything? 8. I am too busy, I cannot wait you. 9. I asked his book. 10. She pointed the ship in the distance.

EXERCISE 89.

Make sentences of your own, using suitable prepositions after the following:

1. Ask. 2. Explain. 3. Knock. 4. Listen. 5. Remind. 6. Say. 7. Search. 8. Speak. 9. Wait. 10. Wish.

UNNECESSARY PREPOSITIONS
(§§ 291–307)

EXERCISE 90.

Use each of the following in a separate sentence:

1. Answer. 2. Attack. 3. Approach. 4. Enter. 5. Obey. 6. Reach. 7. Resemble. 8. Tell. 9. Behind. 10. Inside. 11. Outside. 12. Around.

COMMON MISTAKES IN ENGLISH

EXERCISE 91.

Fill the blanks with prepositions where necessary:

1. Let us play outside — the house. 2. She is searching — her pencil. 3. I waited — him half an hour. 4. We entered — a long discussion. 5. I taught my dog to obey — me. 6. He entered — the house by the back door. 7. Twins resemble — each other. 8. The poor always wish — riches. 9. I told — him the truth. 10. I promised to write — my father.

CONJUNCTIONS

MISCELLANEOUS EXAMPLES

EXERCISE 92.

Correct the following sentences, giving reasons for your corrections:

1. The book is neither green or red. 2. He cannot speak English and French. 3. It costs two, three pounds. 4. He not only spoke loudly, but also clearly. 5. He ate and the three oranges. 6. I counted one hundred seven people. 7. She wants to learn and French. 8. He said that, "You will be sorry for it." 9. I do not know if I shall be able to go. 10. From now and on I will work hard.

ANSWERS TO EXERCISE

1. § 184. 2. § 187. 3. § 281. 4. § 382. 5. § 596. 6. § 280. 7. § 597. 8. § 347. 9. § 181. 10. § 358.

EXERCISES

EXERCISE 93.

Fill each blank with the correct word: **as** or **like**.

1. Act — a gentleman. 2. He does — he pleases. 3. He behaved — a baby. 4. She looks — her mother. 5. Do — he does. 6. Play the game — he does. 7. She dances — a fairy. 8. You walk — he does. 9. He acted just — the rest. 10. He speaks — an Englishman.

EXERCISE 94.

Fill each blank with the correct word: **no** or **not**.

1. I have — time for play. 2. She has — a good memory. 3. He had — reason to be angry. 4. There is — enough furniture in this room. 5. Your plan is — different from mine. 6. I had — patience with him. 7. There were — fewer than a thousand people. 8. There is — furniture in this room. 9. He has — enough money. 10. I want — more, thank you.

EXERCISE 95.

Fill the blanks with the correct word: **died** or **dead**.

1. Her grandfather is —. 2. He — of fever. 3. The — cannot feel. 4. Her aunt is — ; she — many years ago. 5. The man — for his country. 6. The — horse is lying in the field. 7. They — a cruel death. 8. The flowers have —. 9. The soldier — from his wounds. 10. The past is —.

COMMON MISTAKES IN ENGLISH

EXERCISE 96.

Fill each blank with the correct word: **it's** or **its**.

1. The bird has broken — wing. 2. I fear — going to rain. 3. — almost nine o'clock. 4. I think — yours. 5. The tree will soon lose — leaves. 6. — time to go home. 7. Every river has — source. 8. — a long time until Christmas. 9. An animal will often die for — young. 10. — too late to go now.

EXERCISE 97.

Fill each blank with the correct word: **good** or **well**.

1. Mary did her work —. 2. She speaks — English. 3. I did — in the examination. 4. She looks — today. 5. It is — to be with friends. 6. He did — work. 7. He did not see —. 8. Has he done — in his lessons? 9. I am quite —. 10. She speaks very —.

EXERCISE 98.

Fill each blank with the correct word: **past** or **passed.**

1. The — month was rainy. 2. He — his examination. 3. The ball — between the goal-posts. 4. The bullet whistled — my ear. 5. Several months have — since the year began. 6. Forget the —. 7. The aeroplane flew —. 8. It is half — eight. 9. She — the salt to the guest. 10. The door was open when I walked —.

EXERCISES

EXERCISE 99.

Rewrite these sentences, choosing the right word between the brackets:

1. This thing (is, does) not worth more than five pence. 2. (After, then) he shut the door and went to bed. 3. He (is, does) not able to speak English correctly. 4. Don't be (fool, foolish). 5. He is a (fool, foolish). 6. Flowers smell (sweet, sweetly). 7. He is so proud that he does not greet (and, even) his friends. 8. The mother (weighed, weighted) her baby. 9. I want to learn (and) other languages (too). 10. Is it (truth, true)?

GENERAL EXERCISE[1]

Correct whatever is wrong in the following:

1. Why you study the English? (372, 313)
2. John reads good, isn't it? (593, 167)
3. Why you not say the truth? (372, 210)
4. Will I go at the post-office? (406, 389)
5. How to make this problem, sir? (133, 409)
6. Is he more better from me? (348, 156, 138)
7. I have written him last week. (115, 245)
8. I past too well to the hotel. (600, 467, 389)
9. Let me to try to do this and me. (334, 597)
10. I have never seen a so good film. (384, 269)
11. He has not ate nothing these two days. (113, 170)

[1] The numbers in the brackets refer to the sections in which the mistakes are explained.

12. When I sleep I take out my shoes. (448, 458)
13. He did not obeyed to their advices. (105, 299, 530)
14. He is going each morning to the market. (122, 481, 322)
15. He is working in the office since five years. (118, (402)
16. How you are going with your piano lessons? (372, 222)
17. Can you to come for dinner today evening? (329, 223)
18. My brother he is found in the first class. (340, 449)
19. It does not worth to say lies about it. (589, 98, 408).
20. I made all which I could for helping him. (409, 146, 168)
21. It is two years now since he left from England. (119, 298)
22. Please return back to shut the light. (350, 212)
23. Avoid to make these sort of mistakes. (87, 561)
24. Myself and my sister will not be present. (142, 388)
25. He got down from his bicycle and spoke me. (196, 240)
26. He came with the train from the Alexandria. (14, 308)
27. He would not take fewer than hundred pounds. (490, 254)
28. The two first pages of my book has been lost. (383, 570)

29. The knife was laying on the table where I lay it. (410)
30. That punishment will learn him to do not do it again. (438, 369)
31. You neither work at school or at your house. (184, 382, 503)
32. I cannot understand because he don't speak clear. (247, 594)
33. The man which you saw him yesterday is very rich. (145, 344)
34. He said that he has never not gone at London. (108, 170, 389)
35. I think to go to home for to spend the holidays. (84, 360, 354)
36. The office is only open on the morning at Saturday. (366, 393)
37. It is two years since I began to study the English. (119, 313)
38. He told that he was at England before three years. (408, 391, 470)
39. He was angry at me because I said him he has wrong. (6, 408, 108, 190)
40. When I went to home I found that the money was disappeared. (360, 163)
41. He said to me that he is not satisfied from his teacher. (408, 108, 60)
42. He told that he cannot remember nothing about it. (408, 111, 170)
43. I and he intend to leave to England after two weeks. (388, 45, 404)
44. I am knowing my lesson but cannot say it in the English. (121, 313)

45. I rang two times, but I could not make no one to hear. (171, 170, 335)
46. I put a new bell on my bicycle which it cost fifteen pence. (380, 344)
47. When he will return back, I shall say him everything. (127, 350, 408)
48. I am much pleased to inform you that I have reached to this station yesterday. (468, 115, 301)
49. British Isles are consisted from England, Wales, Scotland and Ireland. (308, 20)
50. The English is not only difficult to write it, but also to speak it. (313, 382, 346)

INDEX

The numbers refer to sections. Entries between quotation marks show incorrect forms.

INDEX

INDEX

INDEX

dozens, for **dozen**, 542; use of, 542 (note)

dream, for **dream of**, 229

dress, for **suit**, 519

dress (verb), use of, 416 (note)

"dressed with," 30

"drink a cigarette," etc., 208

drown, for **sink** 443

due to, for **because of**, 575

dust, for **cover with dust**, 434

E

each and **every**, 481

each other and **one another**, 153

either . . . or, use of, 184

else, wrongly omitted in comparisons, 270

engaged to, 48 (note)

enjoy, misuse of infinitive after, 88; object of, wrongly omitted, 278

"enjoy one's time," 278 (note)

enough, position of, 367

enter into, for **enter**, 296; use of, 296 (note)

etc., misuse of, 356 (note)

even, position of, 363

evening, wrongly preceded by **an**, 172

ever, position of, 363

every, for **each**, 481

"everything which," 146

except, for **besides**, 397

"exception of," 31

"exchange by," 32

excuse, misuse of infinitive after, 89

explain, for **explain to**, 230

F

"fail from," 33

fall, for **fell**, 465

far, misuse of, with definite distance, 361

farther and **further**, 486

favourite, use of, 497 (note)

feed on, 46 (note)

"feel . . . to," 339

fell, use of, 465 (note)

fetch, use of, 442 (note)

few and **a few**, 479

fewer, use of, 490

fill with, 34 (note)

finger, for **toe**, 515

finish, misuse of infinitive after, 90

"finish from," 297

fire at, 5 (note)

first two, etc., 383

fishes, for **fish**, 539 (note)

flee, use of, 464 (note)

float, use of, 464 (note)

flown, for **flowed**, 464

"follow a game," etc., 211

fond of, misuse of infinitive after, 79

fool and **foolish**, 574

foot, go on, 14 (note); for **leg**, 514

for, for **about**, 401

for and **at** (price), 394

"for this," 283

"for to," 354

foreigner, use of, 512 (note)

found, for **to be**, 449; for **find**, 466; use of, 466 (note)

friendly, misused as adverb, 579

from, misuse of, with Comparative, 156; for **one of**, 161; for **by**, 399; for **since**, 403; use of, 403 (note)

"from now and on," 358

from where, for **where**, 355

fruits, for **fruit**, 540 (note)

"full with," 34

fun, wrongly preceded by **a**, 328

"furnitures," 532

further, current use of, 486

Future tense, misuse of, in time clause, 127; in **if**-clause, 128

G

gain, use of, 431 (note)

Gender, confusion of, 135

gentleman, for **man**, 520

Gerund, misuse of, 168

"get rid from," 35

"give an examination," 189

INDEX

INDEX

INDEX

INDEX

INDEX

INDEX

INDEX

INDEX

IRREGULAR VERBS

	Present	*Past*	*Past Participle*
61	light	lit	lit
	lose	lost	lost
	make	made	made
	mean	meant	meant
	meet	met	met
	pay	paid	paid
	put	put	put
	read	read	read
	ride	rode	ridden
70	ring	rang	rung
	rise	rose	risen
	run	ran	run
	say	said	said
	see	saw	seen
	seek	sought	sought
	sell	sold	sold
	send	sent	sent
	set	set	set
	sew	sewed	sewn
80	shake	shook	shaken
	shed	shed	shed
	shine	shone	shone
	shoot	shot	shot
	show	showed	shown
	shrink	shrank	shrunk
	shut	shut	shut
	sing	sang	sung
	sink	sank	sunk
	sit	sat	sat
90	sleep	slept	slept